AIR CRASH
INVESTIGATIONS

LOCKERBIE

The Bombing of PANAM
Flight 103

AIR CRASH INVESTIGATIONS

Over the last decades flying has become an every day event, there is nothing special about it anymore. Safety has increased tremendously, but unfortunately accidents still happen. Every accident is a source for improvement. It is therefore essential that the precise cause or probable cause of accidents is as widely known as possible. It can not only take away fear for flying but it can also make passengers aware of unusual things during a flight and so play a role in preventing accidents.

Air Crash Investigation Reports are published by official government entities and can in principle usually be down loaded from the websites of these entities. It is however not always easy, certainly not by foreign countries, to locate the report someone is looking for. Often the reports are accompanied by numerous extensive and very technical specifications and appendices and therefore not easy readable. In this series we have streamlined the reports of a number of important accidents in aviation without compromising in any way the content of the reports in order to make the issue at stake more easily accessible for a wider public.

Allistair Fitzgerald, editor.

AIR CRASH INVESTIGATIONS

LOCKERBIE

The Bombing of PANAM Flight 103

Allistair Fitzgerald, editor

MABUHAY PUBLISHING

4

AIR CRASH INVESTIGATIONS

Report on the accident to
Boeing 747-121, N739PA at
Lockerbie, Dumfriesshire, Scotland
on 21 December 1988

The details of the final *Aircraft Accident Report* of the Air Accidents Investigation Branch, Department of Transport, Air Accidents Investigation Branch Royal Aerospace Establishment Farnborough, United Kingdom, on the circumstances of the accident to Boeing 747-121, N739PA which occurred near the town of Lockerbie, Dumfriesshire, Scotland on 21 December 1988. (Aircraft Accident Report No 2/90, EW/C1094)

A Lulu.com imprint

ISBN: 978-0-557-72932-6

Contents

Air Accidents Investigation Branch

Aircraft Accident Report No. 2/90 (EW/C10940

Operator:		Pan American World Airways
Aircraft	Type:	Boeing 747-121
	Nationality:	United States of America
	Registration:	N 739 PA
Place of Accident		Lockerbie, Dumfries, Scotland
		Latitude: 55° 07¹ N
		Longitude: 003° 21¹ W
Date and Time (UTC)		21 December 1988 at 19.02:50 hrs

All times in this report are UTC

SYNOPSIS

The accident was notified to the Air Accidents Investigation Branch at 19.40 hrs on the 21 December 1988 and the investigation commenced that day. The members of the AAIB team are listed at Appendix A.

The aircraft, Flight PA103 from London Heathrow to New York, had been in level cruising flight at flight level 310 (31,000 feet) for approximately seven minutes when the last secondary radar return was received just before 19.03 hrs. The radar then showed multiple primary returns fanning out downwind. Major portions of the wreckage of the aircraft fell on the town of Lockerbie with other large parts landing in the countryside to the east of the town. Lighter debris from the aircraft was strewn along two trails, the longest of which extended some 130 kilometres to the east coast of England. Within a few days items of wreckage were retrieved upon which forensic scientists found conclusive evidence of a detonating high explosive. The airport security and criminal aspects of the accident are the subject of a separate investigation and are not covered in this report which concentrates on the technical aspects of the disintegration of the aircraft.

The report concludes that the detonation of an improvised explosive device led directly to the destruction of the aircraft with the loss of all 259 persons on board and 11 of the residents of the town of Lockerbie. Five recommendations are made of which four concern flight recorders, including the funding of a study to devise methods of recording violent positive and negative pressure pulses associated with explosions. The final recommendation is that Airworthiness Authorities and aircraft manufacturers undertake a systematic study with a view to identifying measures that might mitigate the effects of explosive devices and improve the tolerance of the aircraft's structure and systems to explosive damage.

FACTUAL INFORMATION

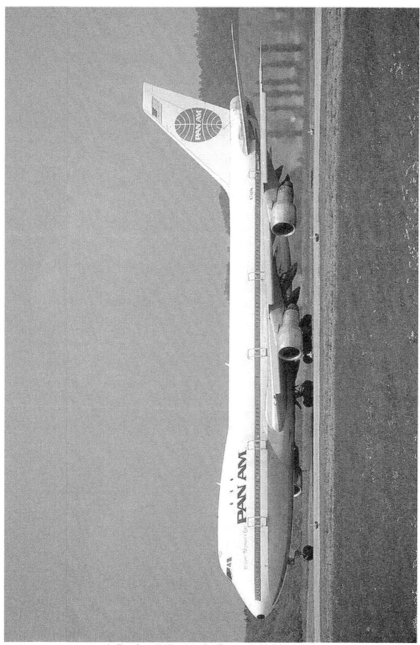

A Boeing 747-100 similar to PANAM 103

CHAPTER 1

THE BASIC FACTS

History of the Flight

Boeing 747, N739PA, arrived at London Heathrow Airport from San Francisco and parked on stand Kilo 14, to the south-east of Terminal 3. Many of the passengers for this aircraft had arrived at Heathrow from Frankfurt, West Germany on a Boeing 727, which was positioned on stand Kilo 16, next to N739PA. These pasengers were transferred with their baggage to N739PA which was to operate the scheduled Flight PA103 to New York Kennedy. Passengers from other flights also joined Flight PA103 at Heathrow. After a 6 hour turnround, Flight PA 103 was pushed back from the stand at 18.04 hrs and was cleared to taxy on the inner taxiway to runway 27R. The only relevant Notam warned of work in progress on the outer taxiway. The departure was unremarkable.

Flight PA103 took-off at 18.25 hrs. As it was approaching the Burnham VOR it took up a radar heading of 350° and flew below the Bovingdon holding point at 6000 feet. It was then cleared to climb initially to flight level (FL) 120 and subsequently to FL 310. The aircraft levelled off at FL 310 north west of Pole Hill VOR at 18.56 hrs. Approximately 7 minutes later, Shanwick Oceanic Control transmitted the aircraft's oceanic clearance but this transmission was not acknowledged. The secondary radar return from Flight PA 103 disappeared from the radar screen during this transmission. Multiple primary radar returns were then seen fanning out downwind for a considerable distance. Debris from the aircraft was strewn along two trails, one of which extended some 130 km to the east coast of England. The upper winds were between 250° and 260° and decreased in strength from 115 kt at FL 320 to 60 kt at FL 100 and 15 to 20 kt at the surface.

Two major portions of the wreckage of the aircraft fell on the town of Lockerbie; other large parts, including the flight deck and forward fuselage section, landed in the countryside to the east of the town. Residents of Lockerbie reported that, shortly after 19.00 hrs, there was a rumbling noise like thunder which rapidly increased to deafening proportions like the roar of a jet engine under power. The noise appeared to come from a meteor-like object which was trailing flame and came down in the north-eastern part of the town. A larger, dark, delta shaped object, resembling an aircraft wing, landed at about the same time in the Sherwood area of the town. The delta shaped object was not on fire while in the air, however, a very large fireball ensued which was of short duration and carried large amounts of debris into the air, the lighter particles being deposited several miles downwind. Other less well defined objects were seen to land in the area.

Injuries to persons

Injuries	Crew	Passengers	Others
Fatal	16	243	11
Serious			2
Minor/None			3

Damage to aircraft

The aircraft was destroyed

Other damage

The wings impacted at the southern edge of Lorkerbie, producing a crater whose volume, calculated from a photogrammetric survey, was approximately 560 cubic metres. The weight of material displaced by the wing impact was estimated to be well in excess of 1500 tonnes. The wing impact created a fireball, setting fire to neighbouring houses and carrying aloft debris which was then blown downwind for several miles. It was subsequently established that domestic properties had been so seriously damaged as a result of fire and/or impact that 21 had to be demolished and an even greater number of homes required substantial repairs. Major portions of the aircraft, including the engines, also landed on the town of Lockerbie and other large parts, including the flight deck and forward fuselage section, landed in the countryside to the east of the town. Lighter debris from the aircraft was strewn as far as the east coast of England over a distance of 130 kilometres.

Personnel Information

Commander

Commander:	Male, aged 55 years
Licence:	USA Airline Transport Pilot's Licence
Aircraft ratings:	Boeing 747, Boeing 707, Boeing 720, Lockheed L1011, and Douglas DC3
Medical Certificate	Class 1,valid to April 1989, with the limitation that the holder shall wear lenses that correct for distant vision and possess glasses that correct for near vision
Flying Experience	Total all types: 10,910 hours Total on type: 4,107 hours Total last 28 days: 82 hours
Duty time	Commensurate with company requirements

Last base check	11 November 1988
Last route check	30 June 1988
Last emergencies check	8 November 1988

Co-pilot

Co-pilot:	Male, 52 years
Licence:	USA Airline Transport Pilot's Licence
Aircraft ratings:	Boeing 747, Boeing 707, Boeing 727
Medical Certificate:	Class 1, valid to April 1989, with the limitation that the holder shall possess correcting glasses for near vision
Flying experience:	Total all types: 11,855 hours
Total on type:	5,517 hours
Total last 28 days:	51 hours
Duty time:	Commensurate with company requirements
Last base check:	30 November 1988
Last route check:	Not required
Last emergencies check:	27 November 1988

Flight Engineer

Flight Engineer:	Male, aged 46 years

Licence: USA Flight Engineer's Licence

Aircraft ratings: Turbojet

Medical certificate: Class 2, valid to June 1989, with the
                                   limitation that the holder shall wear
                                   correcting glasses for near vision

Flying experience: Total all types: 8,068 hours

Total on type: 487 hours

Total last 28 days: 53 hours

Duty time: Commensurate with company
                                   requirements

Last base check: 30 October 1988

Last route check: Not required

Last emergencies check: 27 October 1988

Flight Attendants

Flight Attendants: There were 13 Flight Attendants on the
                                   aircraft, all of whom met company
                                   proficiency and medical requirements

Aircraft information

Leading particulars

Aircraft type: Boeing 747-121

Constructor's serial number: 19646

Engines: 4 Pratt and Whitney JT9D-7A turbofan

General description

The Boeing 747 aircraft, registration N739PA, was a conventionally designed long range transport aeroplane. A diagram showing the general arrangement is shown at Appendix B, Figure B-1 together with the principal dimensions of the aircraft.

The fuselage of the aircraft type was of approximately circular section over most of its length, with the forward fuselage having a diameter of 21 Y4 feet where the cross-section was constant. The pressurised section of the fuselage (which included the forward and aft cargo holds) had an overall length of 190 feet, extending from the nose to a point just forward of the tailplane. In normal cruising flight the service pressure differential was at the miximum value of 8.9 pounds per square inch. The fuselage was of conventional skin, stringer and frame construction, riveted throughout, generally using countersunk flush riveting for the skin panels. The fuselage frames were spaced at 20 inch intervals and given the same numbers as their stations, defined in terms of the distance in inches from the datum point close to the nose of the aircraft [Appendix B, Figure B-2]. The skin panels were joined using vertical butt joints and horizontal lap joints. The horizontal lap joints used three rows of rivets together with a cold bonded adhesive.

Accommodation within the aircraft was predominately on the main deck, which extended throughout the whole length of the pressurised compartment. A separate upper deck was incorporated in the forward part of the aircraft. This upper deck was reached by means of a spiral staircase from the main deck and incorporated the flight crew compartment together with additional passenger accommodation. The cross-section of the forward fuselage differed considerably from the near circular section of the remainder of the aircraft, incorporating an additional smaller radius arc above the upper deck section joined to the main circular arc of the lower cabin portion by elements of straight fuselage frames and flat skin.

In order to preserve the correct shape of the aircraft under pressurisation loading, the straight portions of the fuselage frames in the region of the upper deck floor and above it were required to be much stiffer than the frame portions lower down in the aircraft. These straight sections were therefore of very much more substantial construction than most of the curved sections of frames lower down and further back in the fuselage. There was considerable variation in the gauge of the fuselage skin at various locations in the forward fuselage of the aircraft.

The fuselage structure of N739PA differed from that of the majority of Boeing 747 aircraft in that it had been modified to carry special purpose freight containers on the main deck, in place of seats. This was known as the Civil Reserve Air Fleet (CRAF) modification and enabled the aircraft to be quickly converted for carriage of military freight containers on the main deck during times of national emergency. The effect of this modification on the structure of the fuselage was mainly to replace the existing main deck floor beams with beams of more substantial cross-section than those generally found in passenger carrying Boeing 747 aircraft. A large side loading door, generally known as the CRAF door, was also incorporated on the left side of the main deck aft of the wing.

Below the main deck, in common with other Boeing 747 aircraft, were a number of additional compartments, the largest of which were the forward and aft freight holds used for the storage of cargo and baggage in standard air-transportable containers. These containers were placed within the aircraft hold by means of a freight handling system and were carried on a system of rails approximately 2 feet above the outer skin at the bottom of the aircraft, there being no continuous floor as such, below these baggage containers. The forward freight compartment had a length of approximately 40 feet and a depth of approximately 6 feet. The containers were loaded into the forward hold through a large cargo door on the right side of the aircraft.

Internal fuselage cavities

Because of the conventional skin, frame and stringer type of construction, common to all large public transport aircraft, the fuselage was effectively divided into a series of 'bays'. Each bay, comprising two adjacent fuselage frames and the structure between them, provided, in effect, a series of interlinking cavities bounded by the frames, floor beams, fuselage skins and cabin floor panels etc. The principal cavities thus formed were:

(i)   A semi-circular cavity formed in between the fuselage frames in the lower lobe of the hull, i.e. from the crease beam (at cabin floor level) on one side down to the belly beneath the containers and up to the opposite crease beam, bounded by the fuselage skin on the outside and the containers/cargo liner on the inside [Appendix B, Figure B-3, detail A].

(ii)   A horizontal cavity between the main cabin floor beams, the cabin floor panels and the cargo bay liner. This extended the full width of the fuselage and linked the upper ends of the lower lobe cavity [Appendix B, Figure B3, detail B].

(iii)   A narrow vertical cavity between the two containers [Appendix B, Figure B-3, detail C].

(iv)   A further narrow cavity around the outside of the two containers, between the container skins and the cargo bay liner, communicating with the lower lobe cavity [Appendix B, Figure B-3, detail D].

(v)   A continuation of the semi-circular cavity into the space behind the cabin wall liner [Appendix B, Figure B-3, detail E]. This space was restricted somewhat by the presence of the window assembly, but nevertheless provided a continuous cavity extending upwards to the level of the upper deck floor. Forward of station 740, this cavity was effectively terminated at its upper end by the presence of diaphragms which formed extensions of the upper deck floor panels; aft of station 740, the cavity communicated with the ceiling space and the cavity in the fuselage crown aft of the upper deck.

All of these cavities were repeated at each fuselage bay (formed between pairs of fuselage frames), and all of the cavities in a given bay were linked together, principally at the crease beam area [Appendix B, Figure B-3, region F]. Furthermore, each of the set of bay cavities was linked with the next by the longitudinal cavities formed between the cargo hold liner and the outer hull, just below the crease beam [Appendix B, Figure B-3, detail F]; i.e. this cavity formed a manifold linking together each of the bays within the cargo hold.

The main passenger cabin formed a large chamber which communicated directly with each of the sub floor bays, and also with the longitudinal manifold cavity, via the air conditioning and cabin/cargo bay de-pressurisation vent passages in the crease beam area. (It should be noted that a similar communication did not exist between the upper and lower cabins because there were no air conditioning/depressurisation passages to bypass the upper deck floor.)

Aircraft weight and centre of gravity

Loading:	lb	kg
Operating empty weight	366,228	166,120
Additional crew	130	59
243 passengers (1)	40,324	18,291
Load in compartments:		
1	11,616	5,269
2	20,039	9,090
3	15,057	6,830
4	17,196	7,800
5	2,544	1,154
Total in compartments (2)	66,452	30,143
Total traffic load	106,776	48,434
Zero fuel weight	472,156	214,554
Fuel (Take-off)	239,997	108,862
Actual take-off weight(4)	713,002	323,416
Maximum take-off weight	733,992	332,937

Note 1: Calculated at standard weights and including cabin baggage.

Note 2: Despatch information stated that the cargo did not include dangerous goods, perishable cargo, live animals or known security exceptions.

Maintenance details

N739PA first flew in 1970 and spent its whole service life in the hands of Pan American World Airways Incorporated. Its Certificate of Airworthiness was issued on 12 February 1970 and remained in force until the time of the accident, at which time the aircraft had completed a total of 72,464 hours flying and 16,497 flight cycles. Details of the last 4 maintenance checks carried out during the aircraft's life are shown below:

DATE	SERVICE	HOURS	CYCLES
27 Sept 88	C Check (Interior upgrade)	71,502	16,347
2 Nov 88	B Service Check	71,919	16,406
27 Nov 88	Base 1	72,210	16,454
13 Dec 88	Base 2	72,374	16,481

The CRAF modification programme was undertaken in September 1987. At the same time a series of modifications to the forward fuselage from the nose back to station 520 (Section 41) were carried out to enable the aircraft to continue in service without a continuing requirement for structural inspections in certain areas.

All Airworthiness Directives relating to the Boeing 747 fuselage structure between stations 500 and 1000 have been reviewed and their applicability to this aircraft checked. In addition, Service Bulletins relating to the structure in this area were also reviewed. The applicable Service Bulletins, some of which implement the Airworthiness Directives are listed below together with their subjects. The dates, total aircraft times and total aircraft cycles at which each relevant inspection was last carried out have been reviewed and their status on aircraft N739PA at the time of the accident has been established.

N739PA Service Bulletin compliance:

SB 53-2064   Front Spar Pressure Bulkhead Chord Reinforcement and Drag Splice Fitting Rework.

Modification accomplished on 6 July 1974. Post-modification repetitive inspection IAW (in accordance with) AD 84-18-06 last accomplished on 19 November 1985 at 62,030 TAT hours (Total Aircraft Time) and 14,768 TAC (Total Aircraft Cycles).

SB 53-2088	Frame to Tension Tie Joint Modification - BS760 to 780. Repetitive inspection IAW AD 84-19-01 last accomplished on 19 June 1985 at 60,153 hours TAT and 14,436 TAC.
SB 53-2200	Lower Cargo Doorway Lower Sill Truss and Latch Support Fitting Inspection Repair and Replacement. Repetitive inspection IAW AD 79-17-02 R2 last accomplished 2 November 1988 at 71,919 hours TAT and 16,406 TAC.
SB 53-2234	Fuselage - Auxiliary Structure - Main Deck Floor - BS 480Floor Beam Upper Chord Modification. Repetitive inspection per SB 53A2263 IAW AD 86-23-06 last accomplished on 26 September 1987 at 67,376 hours TAT and 15,680 TAC.
SB 53-2237	Fuselage - Main Frame - BS 540 thru 760 and 1820 thru 1900 Frame Inspection and Reinforcement. Repetitive inspection IAW AD 86-18-01 last accomplished on 27 February 1987 at 67,088 hours TAT and 15,627 TAC.
SB 53-2267	Fuselage - Skin - Lower Body Longitudinal Skin Lap Jointand Adjacent Body Frame Inspection and Repair. Terminating modification accomplished 100% under wing-to-

body fairings and approximately 80%
in forward and aft fuselage sections
on 26 September 1987 at 67,376
hours TAT and 15,680 TAC.
Repetitive inspection of unmodified
lap joints JAW AD 8609-07 R1 last
accomplished on 18 August 1988 at
71,043 hours TAT and 16,273 TAC.

SB 53A2303

Fuselage - Nose Section - station 400
to 520 Stringer 6 Skin Lap Splice
Inspection, Repair and Modification.
Repetitive inspection JAW AD 89-
05-03 last accomplished on 26
September 1987 at 67,376 hours
TAT and 15,680 TAC.

This documentation, when viewed together with the detailed content
of the above service bulletins, shows the aircraft to have been in
compliance with the requirements laid down in each of those
bulletins. Some maintenance items were outstanding at the time the
aircraft was despatched on the last flight, however, none of these
items relate to the structure of the aircraft and none had any
relevance to the accident.

Meteorological Information

General weather conditions

An aftercast of the general weather conditions in the area of
Lockerbie at about 19.00 hrs was obtained from the Meteorological
Office, Bracknell. The synoptic situation included a warm sector
covering northern England and most of Scotland with a cold front
some 200 nautical miles to the west of the area moving eastwards
at about 35 knots. The weather consisted of intermittent rain or
showers. The cloud consisted of 4 to 6 oktas of stratocumulus
based at 2,200 feet with 2 oktas of altocumulus between 15,000 and

18,000 feet. Visibility was over 15 kilometers and the freezing level was at 8,500 feet with a sub-zero layer between 4,000 and 5,200 feet.

Winds

There was a weakening jet stream of around 115 knots above Flight Level 310. From examination of the wind profile (see below), there appeared to be insufficient shear both vertically and horizontally to produce any clear air turbulence but there may have been some light turbulence.

Flight Level	Wind
320	260°/115 knots
300	260°/ 90 knots
240	250°/ 80 knots
180	260°/ 60 knots
100	250°/ 60 knots
050	260°/ 40 knots
Surface	240°/ 15 to 20 gusting 25 to 30 knots

Communications

The aircraft communicated normally on London Heathrow aerodrome, London control and Scottish control frequencies. Tape recordings and transcripts of all radio telephone (RTF) communications on these frequencies were available.

At 18.58 hrs the aircraft established two-way radio contact with Shanwick Oceanic Area Control on frequency 123.95 MHz. At 19.02:44 hrs the clearance delivery officer at Shanwick transmitted to the aircraft its oceanic route clearance. The aircraft did not acknowledge this message and made no subsequent transmission.

ATC recording replay

Scottish Air Traffic Control provided copy tapes with time injection for both Shanwick and Scottish ATC frequencies. The source of the time injection on the tapes was derived from the British Telecom "TIM" signal.

The tapes were replayed and the time signals corrected for errors at the time of the tape mounting.

Analysis of ATC tape recordings

From the cockpit voice recorder (CVR) tape it was known that Shanwick was transmitting Flight PA103's transatlantic clearance when the CVR stopped. By synchronising the Shanwick tape and the CVR it was possible to establish that a loud sound was heard on the CVR cockpit area microphone (CAM) channel at 19.02:50 hrs ±1 second.

As the Shanwick controller continued to transmit Flight PA103's clearance instructions through the initial destruction of the aircraft it would not have been possible for a distress call to be received from N739PA on the Shanwick frequency. The Scottish frequency tape recording was listened to from 19.02 hrs until 19.05 hrs for any unexplained sounds indicating an attempt at a distress call but none was heard.

A detailed examination and analysis of the ATC recording together with the flight recorder, radar, and seismic recordings is contained in Appendix C.

Flight recorders

The Digital Flight Data Recorder (DFDR) and the Cockpit Voice Recorder (CVR) were found close together at UK Ordnance Survey (OS) Grid Reference 146819, just to the east of Lockerbie, and recovered approximately 15 hours after the accident. Both recorders were taken directly to AAIB Farnborough for replay. Details of the examination and analysis of the flight recorders together with the radar, ATC and seismic recordings are contained in Appendix C.

Digital flight data recorder

The flight data recorder installation conformed to ARINC 573B standard with a Lockheed Model 209 DFDR receiving data from a Teledyne Controls Flight Data Acquisition Unit (FDAU). The system recorded 22 parameters and 27 discrete (event) parameters. The flight recorder control panel was located in the flight deck overhead panel. The FDAU was in the main equipment centre at the front end of the forward hold and the flight recorder was mounted in the aft equipment centre.

Decoding and reduction of the data from the accident flight showed that no abnormal behaviour of the data sensors had been recorded and that the recorder had simply stopped at 19.02:50 hrs $\pm$1 second.

Cockpit voice recorder

The aircraft was equipped with a 30 minute duration 4 track Fairchild Model A100 CVR, and a Fairchild model A152 cockpit area microphone (CAM). The CVR control panel containing the CAM was located in the overhead panel on the flight deck and the recorder itself was mounted in the aft equipment centre.

The channel allocation was as follows:-

> Channel 1 Flight Engineer's RTF.
> Channel 2 Co-Pilot's RTF.
> Channel 3 Pilot's RTF.
> Channel 4 Cockpit Area Microphone.

The erase facility within the CVR was not functioning satisfactorily and low level communications from earlier recordings were audible on the RTF channels. The CAM channel was particularly noisy, probably due to the combination of the inherently noisy flight deck of the B747-100 in the climb and distortion from the incomplete erasure of the previous recordings. On two occasions the crew had difficulty understanding ATC, possibly indicating high flight deck noise levels. There was a low frequency sound present at irregular intervals on the CAM track but the source of this sound could not be identified and could have been of either acoustic or electrical origin.

The CVR tape was listened to for its full duration and there was no indication of anything abnormal with the aircraft, or unusual crew behaviour. The tape record ended, at 19.02:50 hrs ±1 second, with a sudden loud sound on the CAM channel followed almost immediately by the cessation of recording whilst the crew were copying their transatlantic clearance from Shanwick ATC.

CHAPTER 2

WRECKAGE AND IMPACT INFORMATION

General distribution of wreckage in the field

The complete wing primary structure, incorporating the centre section, impacted at the southern edge of Lockerbie. Major portions of the aircraft, including the engines, also landed in the town. Large portions of the aircraft fell in the countryside to the east of the town and lighter debris was strewn to the east as far as the North Sea. The wreckage was distributed in two trails which became known as the northern and southern trails respectively and these are shown in Appendix B, Figure B-4. A computer database of approximately 1200 significant items of wreckage was compiled and included a brief description of each item and the location where it was found

Appendix B, Figures B-5 to B-8 shows photographs of a model of the aircraft on which the fracture lines forming the boundaries of the separate items of structure have been marked. The model is colour coded to illustrate the way in which the wreckage was distributed between the town of Lockerbie and the northern and southern trails.

The crater

The aircraft wing impacted in the Sherwood Crescent area of the town leaving a crater approximately 47 metres (155 feet) long with a volume calculated to be 560 cubic metres.

The projected distance, measured parallel from one leading edge to the other wing tip, of the Boeing 747-100 was approximately 143 feet, whereas the span is known to be 196 feet. This suggests that impact took place with the wing structure yawed. Although the depth of the crater varied from one end to the other, its widest part was clearly towards the western end suggesting that the wing structure impacted whilst orientated with its root and centre section to the west.

The work carried out at the main crater was limited to assessing the general nature of its contents. The total absence of debris from the wing primary structure found remote from the crater confirmed the initial impression that the complete wing box structure had been present at the main impact.

The items of wreckage recovered from or near the crater are coloured grey on the model at Appendix B, Figures B-5 to B-8.

The Rosebank Crescent site

A 60 feet long section of fuselage between frame 1241 (the rear spar attachment) and frame 1960 (level with the rear edge of the CRAF cargo door) fell into a housing estate at Rosebank Crescent, just over 600 metres from the crater. This section of the fuselage was that situated immediately aft of the wing, and adjoined the wing and fuselage remains which produced the crater. It is colour coded yellow on the model at Appendix B, Figures B-5 to B-8. All fuselage skin structure above floor level was missing except for the following items:

> Section containing 3 windows between door 4L and CRAF door;
> The CRAF door itself (latched) apart from the top area containing the hinge;

Window belt containing 8 windows aft of 4R door aperture
Window belt containing 3 windows forward of 4R door aperture; Door 4R.

Other items found in the wreckage included both body landing gears, the right wing landing gear, the left and right landing gear support beams and the cargo door (frames 1800-1920) which was latched. A number of pallets, luggage containers and their contents were also recovered from this site.

Forward fuselage and flight deck section.

The complete fuselage forward of approximately station 480 (left side) to station 380 (right side) and incorporating the flight deck and nose landing gear was found as a single piece [Appendix B, Figure B-9] in a field approximately 4 km miles east of Lockerbie at OS Grid Reference 174808. It was evident from the nature of the impact damage and the ground marks that it had fallen almost flat on its left side but with a slight nose-down attitude and with no discernible horizontal velocity. The impact had caused almost complete crushing of the structure on the left side. The radome and right nose landing gear door had detached in the air and were recovered in the southern trail.

Examination of the torn edges of the fuselage skin did not indicate the presence of any pre-existing structural or material defects which could have accounted for the separation of this section of the fuselage. Equally so, there were no signs of explosive blast damage or sooting evident on any part of the structure or the interior fittings. It was noted however that a heavy, semi-eliptical scuff mark was present on the lower right side of the fuselage at approximately station 360. This was later matched to the intake profile of the No 3 engine.

The status of the controls and switches on the flight deck was consistent with normal operation in cruising flight. There were no indications that the crew had attempted to react to rapid decompression or loss of control or that any emergency preparations had been actioned prior to the catastrophic disintegration.

Northern trail

The northern trail was seen to be narrow and clearly defined, to emanate from a point very close to the main impact crater and to be orientated in a direction which agreed closely with the mean wind aftercast for the height band from sea level to 20,000 ft. Also at the western end of the northern trail were the lower rear fuselage at Rosebank Crescent, and the group of Nos. 1, 2 and 4 engines which fell in Lockerbie.

The trail contained items of structure distributed throughout its length, from the area slightly east of the crater, to a point approximately 16 km east, beyond which only items of low weight / high drag such as insulation, interior trim, paper etc, were found. For all practical purposes this trail ended at a range of 25 km.

The northern trail contained mainly wreckage from the rear fuselage, fin and the inner regions of both tailplanes together with structure and skin from the upper half of the fuselage forward to approximately the wing mid-chord position. A number of items from the wing were also found in the northern trail, including all 3 starboard Kreuger flaps, most of the remains of the port Kreuger flaps together with sections of their leading edge attachment structures, one portion of outboard aileron approximately 10 feet long, the aft ends of the flap-track fairings (one with a slide raft wrapped around it), and fragments of glass reinforced plastic honeycombe structure believed to be from the flap system, i.e. fore-flaps, aft-flaps, mid-flaps or adjacent fairings. In addition, a number of pieces of the engine cowlings and both HF antennae (situated projecting aft from the wing-tips) were found in this trail.

All items recovered from the northern trail, with the exception of the wing, engines, and lower rear fuselage in Rosebank Crescent, are coloured red on the model of the aircraft in Appendix B, Figures B-5 to B-8.

Southern trail

The southern trail was easily defined, except within 12 km of Lockerbie where it tended to merge with the northern trail. Further east, it extended across southern Scotland and northern England, essentially in a straight band as far as the North Sea. Most of the significant items of wreckage were found in this trail within a range of 30 km from the main impact crater. Items recovered from the southern trail are coloured green on the model of the aircraft at Appendix B, Figures B-5 to B-8.

The trail contained numerous large items from the forward fuselage. The flight deck and nose of the aircraft fell in the curved part of this trail close to Lockerbie. Fragments of the whole of the left tailplane and the outboard portion of the right tailplane were distributed almost entirely throughout the southern trail. Between 21 and 27 km east of the main impact point (either side of Langholm) substantial sections of tailplane skin were found, some bearing distinctive signs of contact with debris moving outwards and backwards relative to the fuselage. Also found in this area were numerous isolated sections of fuselage frame, clearly originating from the crown region above the forward upper deck.

Datum line

All grid references relating to items bearing actual explosive evidence, together with those attached to heavily distorted items found to originate immediately adjacent to them on the structure, were plotted on an Ordanance Survey (OS) chart. These references, 11 in total, were all found to be distributed evenly about about a mean line orientated 079°(Grid) within the southern trail and were spread over a distance of 12 km. The distance of each reference from the line was measured in a direction parallel to the aircraft's track and all were found to be within 500 metres of the line, with 50% of them being within 250 metres of the line. This line is referred to as the datum line and is shown in Appendix B, Figure B-4.

Distribution of wreckage within the southern trail

North of the datum line and parallel to it were drawn a series of lines at distances of 250, 300, 600 and 900 metres respectively from the line, again measured in a direction parallel to the aircraft's track. The positions on the aircraft structure of specific items of wreckage, for which grid references were known with a high degree of confidence, within the bands formed between these lines, are shown in Appendix B, Figures B-10 to 13. In addition, a separate assessment of the grid references of tailplane and elevator wreckage established that these items were distributed evenly about the 600 metre line.

Area between trails

Immediately east of the crater, the southern trail converged with the northern trail such that, to an easterly distance of approximately 5 km, considerable wreckage existed which could have formed part of either trail. Further east, between 6 and 11 km from the crater, a small number of sections and fragments of the fin had fallen outside the southern boundary of the northern trail. Beyond this a large area existed between the trails in which there was no wreckage.

Examination of wreckage at CAD Longtown

The debris from all areas was recovered by the Royal Air Force to the Army Central Ammunition Depot Longtown, about 20 miles from Lockerbie. Approximately 90% of the hull wreckage was successfully recovered, identified, and laid out on the floor in a two-dimensional reconstruction [Appendix B, Figure B-14]. Baggage container material was incorporated into a full three-dimensional reconstruction. Items of wreckage added to the reconstructions was given a reference number and recorded on a computer database together with a brief description of the item and the location where it was found.

Fuselage

The reconstruction revealed the presence of damage consistent with an explosion on the lower fuselage left side in the forward cargo bay area. A small region of structure bounded approximately by frames 700 & 720 and stringers 38L & 40L, had clearly been shattered and blasted through by material exhausting directly from an explosion centred immediately inboard of this location. The material from this area, hereafter referred to as the 'shatter zone', was mostly reduced to very small fragments, only a few of which were recovered, including a strip of two skins [Appendix B, Figure B-15] forming part of the lap joint at the stringer 39L position.

Surrounding the shatter zone were a series of much larger panels of torn fuselage skin which formed a 'star-burst' fracture pattern around the shatter zone. Where these panels formed the boundary of the shatter zone, the metal in the immediate locality was ragged, heavily distorted, and the inner surfaces were pitted and sooted - rather as if a very large shotgun had been fired at the inner surface of the fuselage at close range. In contrast, the star-burst fractures, outside the boundary of the shatter zone, displayed evidence of more typical overload tearing, though some tears appeared to be rapid and, in the area below the missing panels, were multi-branched. These surrounding skin panels were moderately sooted in the regions adjacent to the shatter zone, but otherwise were lightly sooted or free of soot altogether. (Forensic analysis of the soot deposits on frame and skin material from this area confirmed the presence of explosive residues.) All of these skin panels had pulled away from the supporting structure and had been bent and torn in a manner which indicated that, as well as fracturing in the star burst pattern, they had also petalled outwards producing characteristic, tight curling of the sheet material.

Sections of frames 700 and 720 from the area of the explosion were also recovered and identified. Attached to frame 720 were the remnants of a section of the aluminium baggage container (side) guide rail, which was heavily distorted and displayed deep pitting together with very heavy sooting, indicating that it had been very close to the explosive charge. The pattern of distortion and damage on the frames and guide rail segment matched the overall pattern of damage observed on the skins.

The remainder of the structure forming the cargo deck and lower hull was, generally, more randomly distorted and did not display the clear indications of explosive processes which were evident on the skin panels and frames nearer the focus of the explosion. Nevertheless, the overall pattern of damage was consistent with the propagation of explosive pressure fronts away from the focal area inboard of the shatter zone. This was particularly evident in the fracture and bending characteristics of several of the fuselage frames ahead of, and behind station 700.

The whole of the two-dimensional fuselage reconstruction was examined for general evidence of the mode of disintegration and for signs of localised damage, including overpressure damage and pre-existing damage such as corrosion or fatigue. There was some evidence of corrosion and dis-bonding at the cold-bond lap joints in the fuselage. However, the corrosion was relatively light and would not have compromised significantly the static strength of the airframe. Certainly, there was no evidence to suggest that corrosion had affected the mode of disintegration, either in the area of the explosion or at areas more remote. Similarly, there were no indications of fatigue damage except for one very small region of fatigue, involving a single crack less than 3 inches long, which was remote from the bomb location. This crack was not in a critical area and had not coincided with a fracture path.

No evidence of overpressure fracture or distortion was found at the rear pressure bulkhead. Some suggestion of 'quilting' or 'pillowing' of skin panels between stringers and frames, indicative of localised overpressure, was evident on the skin panels attached to the larger segments of lower fuselage wreckage aft of the blast area. In addition, the mode of failure of the butt joint at station 520 suggested that there had been a rapid overpressure load in this area, causing the fastener heads to 'pop' in the region of stringers 13L to 16L, rather than producing shear in the fasteners. Further evidence of localised overpressure damage remote from the source of the explosion was found during the full three-dimensional reconstruction, detailed later in paragraph 1.12.3.2.

An attempt was made to analyse the fractures, to determine the direction and sequence of failure as the fractures propagated away from the region of the explosion. It was found that the directions of most of the fractures close to the explosion could be determined from an analysis of the fracture surfaces and other features, such as rivet and rivet hole distortions. However, it was apparent that beyond the boundary of the petalled region, the disintegration process had involved multiple fractures taking place simultaneously - extremely complex parallel processes which made the sequencing of events not amenable to conventional analysis.

Wing structure and adjacent fuselage area

On completion of the initial layout at Longtown it became evident that, in the area from station 1000 to approximately station 1240 the only identifiable fuselage structure consisted of elements of fuselage skin, stringers and frames from above the cabin window belts. The wreckage from in and around the crater was therefore sifted to establish more accurately what sections of the aircraft had produced the crater. All of the material was highly fragmented, but it was confirmed that the material comprised mostly wing structure, with a few fragments of fuselage sidewall and passenger seats. The badly burnt state of these fragments made it clear that they were recovered from the area of the main impact crater, the only scene of significant ground fire. Amongst these items a number of cabin window forgings were recovered with sections of thick horizontal panelling attached having a length equivalent to the normal window spacing/frame pitch. This arrangement, with skins of this thickness, is unique to the area from station 1100 to 1260. It is therefore reasonable to assume that these fragments formed parts of the missing cabin sides from station 1000 to station 1260, which must have remained attached to the wing centre section at the time of its impact. Because of the high degree of fragmentation and the relative insignificance of the wing in terms of the overall explosive damage pattern, a reconstruction of the wing material was not undertaken. The sections of the aircraft which went into the crater are colour coded grey in Appendix B, Figures B-5 to B-8.

Fin and aft section of fuselage

Examination of the structure of the fin revealed evidence of in-flight damage to the leading edge caused by the impact of structure or cabin contents. This damage was not severe or extensive and the general break-up of the fin did not suggest either a single readily defined loading direction, or break-up due to the effects of leading edge impact. A few items of fin debris were found between the northern and southern trails.

A number of sections of fuselage frame found in the northern trail exhibited evidence of plastic deformation of skin attachment cleats and tensile overload failure of the attachment rivets. This damage was consistent with that which would occur if the skin had been locally subjected to a high loading in a direction normal to its plane. Although this was suggestive of an internal overpressure condition, the rear fuselage revealed no other evidence to support this possibility. Examination of areas of the forward fuselage known to have been subjected to high blast overpressures revealed no comparable evidence of plastic deformation in the skin attachment cleats or rivets, most skin attachment failures appearing to have been rapid.

Calculations made on the effects of internal pressure generated by an open ended fuselage descending at the highest speed likely to have been experienced revealed that this could not generate an internal pressure approaching that necessary to cause failure in an intact cabin structure.

Baggage containers

During the wreckage recovery operation it became apparent that some items, identified as parts of baggage containers, exhibited damage consistent with being close to a detonating high explosive. It was therefore decided to segregate identifiable container parts and reconstruct any that showed evidence of explosive damage. It was evident, from the main wreckage layout, that the explosion had occurred in the forward cargo hold and, although all baggage container wreckage was examined, only items from this area which showed the relevant characteristics were considered for the reconstruction. Discrimination between forward and rear cargo hold containers was relatively straightforward as the rear cargo hold wreckage was almost entirely confined to Lockerbie, whilst that from the forward hold was scattered along the southern wreckage trail.

All immediately identifiable parts of the forward cargo containers were segregated into areas designated by their serial numbers and items not identified at that stage were collected into piles of similar parts for later assessment. As a result of this two adjacent containers, one of metal construction the other fibreglass, were identified as exhibiting damage likely to have been caused by the explosion. Those parts which could be positively identified as being from these two containers were assembled onto one of three simple wooden frameworks, one each for the floor and superstructure of the metal container and one for the superstructure of the fibreglass container. From this it was positively determined that the explosion had occurred within the metal container (serial number AVE 4041 PA), the direct effects of this being evident also on the forward face of the adjacent fibreglass container (serial number AVN 7511 PA) and on the local airframe on the left side of the aircraft in the region of station 700. It was therefore confirmed that this metal container had been loaded in position 14L in agreement with the aircraft loading records. While this work was in progress a buckled section of the metal container skin was found by an AAIB Inspector to contain, trapped within its folds, an item which was subsequently identified by forensic scientists at the Royal Armaments Research and

42

Development Establishment (RARDE) as belonging to a specific type of radio-cassette player and that this had been fitted with an improvised explosive device (IED).

The reconstruction of these containers and their relationship to the aircraft structure is described in detail in Appendix F. Examination of all other components of the remaining containers revealed only damage consistent with ejection into the high speed slipstream and/or ground impact, and that only one device had detonated within the containers on board the aircraft.

Fuselage three-dimensional reconstruction

The reconstruction

The two-dimensional reconstruction successfully established that there had been an explosion in the forward hold; its location was established and the general damage characteristics in the vicinity of the explosion were determined. However, the mechanisms by which the failure process developed from local damage in the immediate vicinity of the explosion to the complete structural break-up and separation of the whole forward section of the fuselage, could not be adequately investigated without recourse to a more elaborate reconstruction.

To facilitate this additional work, wreckage forming a 65 foot section of the fuselage (approximately 30 feet each side of the explosion) was transported to AAIB Farnborough, where it was attached to a specially designed framework to form a fully three-dimensional reconstruction [Appendix B, Figures B-16 and B17] of the complete fuselage between stations 360 & 1000 (from the separated nose section back to the wing cut out). The support framework was designed to provide full and free access to all parts of the structure, both internally and externally. Because of height constraints, the reconstruction was carried out in two parts, with the structure divided along a horizontal line at approximately the upper cabin floor level. The previously reconstructed containers were also

43

transported to AAIB Farnborough to allow correlation of evidence with, and partial incorporation into, the fuselage reconstruction.

Structure and skin panels were attached to the supporting framework by their last point of attachment, to provide a better appreciation of the modes and direction of curling, distortion, and ultimate separation. Thus, the panels of skin which had petalled back from the shatter zone were attached at their outer edges, so as to identify the bending modes of the panels, the extent of the petalled region, and also the size of the resulting aperture in the hull. In areas more remote from the explosion, the fracture and tear directions were used together with distortion and curling directions to determine the mode of separation, and thus the most appropriate point of attachment to the reconstruction. Cabin floor beam segments were supported on a steel mesh grid and a plot of the beam fractures is shown at Appendix B, Figure B-18.

The cargo container base elements were separated from the rest of the container reconstruction and transferred to the main wreckage reconstruction, where the reassembled container base was positioned precisely onto the cargo deck. To assist in the correlation of the initial shatter zone and petalled-out regions with the position of the explosive device, the boundaries of the skin panel fractures were marked on a transparent plastic panel which was then attached to the reconstruction to provide a transparent pseudo-skin showing the positions of the skin tear lines. This provided a clear visual indication of the relationship between the skin panel fractures and the explosive damage to the container base, thus providing a more accurate indication of the location of the explosive device.

Summary of explosive features evident

The three-dimensional reconstruction provided additional information about the region of tearing and petalling around the shatter zone. It also identified a number of other regions of structural damage, remote from the explosion, which were clearly associated with severe and rapidly applied pressure loads acting normal to the skin's internal surface. These were sufficiently sharp-edged to pre-empt the resolution of pressure induced loads into membrane tension stresses in the skin: instead, the effect was as though these areas of skin had been struck a severe 'pressure blow' from within the hull.

The two types of damage, i.e. the direct blast/tearing/petalling damage and the quite separate areas of 'pressure blow' damage at remote sites were evidently caused by separate mechanisms, though it was equally clear that each was caused by explosive processes, rather than more general disintegration.

The region of petalling was bounded (approximately) by frames 680 and 740, and extended from just below the window belt down nearly to the keel of the aircraft [Appendix B, Figure B-19, region A]. The resulting aperture measured approximately 17 feet by 5 feet. Three major fractures had propagated beyond the boundary of the petalled zone, clearly driven by a combination of hull pressurisation loading and the relatively long term (secondary) pressure pulse from the explosion. These fractures ran as follows:

(i) rearwards and downward in a stepped fashion, joining the stringer 38L lap joint at around station 840, running aft along stringer 38L to around station 920, then stepping down to stringer 39L and running aft to terminate at the wing box cut-out [Appendix B, Figure B-19, fracture 1].

(ii) downwards and forward to join the stringer 44L lap joint, then running forward along stringer 44L as far as station 480 [Appendix B, Figure B-19, fracture 2].

(iii) downwards and rearward, joining the butt line at station 740 to run under the fuselage and up the right side to a position approximately 18 inches above the cabin floor level [Appendix B, Figures B-19 and B-20, fracture 3].

The propagation of tears upwards from the shatter zone appeared to have taken the form of a series of parallel fractures running upwards together before turning towards each other and closing, forming large flaps of skin which appear to have separated relatively cleanly.

Regions of skin separation remote from the site of the explosion were evident in a number of areas. These principally were:

(i)   A large section of upper fuselage skin extending from station 500 back to station 760, and from around stringers 15/19L up as far as stringer 5L [Appendix B, Figures B-19 and B-20, region B], and probably extending further up over the crown. This panel had separated initially at its lower forward edge as a result of a pressure blow type of impulse loading, which had popped the heads from the rivets at the butt joint on frame 500 and lifted the skin flap out into the airflow. The remainder of the panel had then torn away rearwards in the airflow.

A region of 'quilting' or 'pillowing', i.e. spherical bulging of skin panels between frames and stringers, was evident on these panels in the region between station 560 and 680, just below the level of the upper deck floor, indicative of high internal pressurisation loading [Appendix B, Figure B-19, region C[.

(ii)   A smaller section of skin between stations 500 and 580, bounded by stringers 27L and 34L [Appendix B, Figure B-19, region D], had also been 'blown' outwards at its forward edge and torn off the structure rearwards. A characteristic curling of the panel was evident, consistent with rapid, energetic separation from the structure.

(iii)   A section of thick belly skin extending from station 560, stringers 40R to 44R, and tapering back to a point at stringer 45R/station 720 [Appendix B, Figure B-19 and B-20, region E], had separated from the structure as a result of a very heavy 'pressure blow' load at its forward end which had popped the heads off a large number of substantial skin fasteners. The panel had then torn away rearwards from the structure, curling up tightly onto itself as it did so - indicating that considerable excess energy was involved in the separation process (over and above that needed simply to separate the skin material from its supporting structure).

(iv)   A panel of skin on the right side of the aircraft, roughly opposite the explosion, had been torn off the frames, beginning at the top edge of the panel situated just below the window belt and tearing downwards towards the belly [Appendix B, Figure B-20, region F]. This panel was curled downwards in a manner which suggested significant excess energy.

Appendix B, Figure B-21 shows a plot of the fractures noted in the fuselage skins between stations 360 and 1000.

The cabin floor structure was badly disrupted, particularly in the general area above the explosion, where the floor beams had suffered localised upward loading sufficient to fracture them, and the floor panels were missing. Elsewhere, floor beam damage was mainly limited to fractures at the outer ends of the beams and at the centreline, leaving sections of separated floor structure comprising a number of half beams joined together by the Nomex honeycomb floor panels.

General damage features not directly associated with explosive forces

A number of features appeared to be a part of the general structural break-up which followed on from the explosive damage, rather than being a part of the explosive damage process itself. This general break-up was complex and, to a certain extent, random. However, analysis of the fractures, surface scores, paint smears and other features enabled a number of discreet elements of the break-up process to be identified. These elements are summarised below.

(i)   Buckling of the window belts on both sides of the aircraft was evident between stations 660 and 800. That on the left side appeared to be the result of in-plane bending in a nose up sense, followed by fracture. The belt on the right side had a large radius curve suggesting lateral deflection of the fuselage possibly accompanied by some longitudinal compression. This terminated in a peeling failure of the riveted joint at station 800.

(ii)   On the left side three fractures, apparently resulting from in-plane bending/buckling distortion, had traversed the window belt [Appendix B, Figure B-21, detail G]. Of these, the forward two had broken through the window apertures and the aft fracture had exploited a rivet line at the region of reinforcement just forward of the L2 door aperture. On the right side, the window belt had peeled rearwards, after buckling had occurred, separating from the rest of the fuselage, following rivet failure, at the forward edge of the R2 door aperture.

(iii)   All crown skins forward of frame 840 were badly distorted and a number of pieces were missing. It was clearly evident that the skin sections from this region had struck the empennage and/or other structure following separation.

(iv)   The fuselage left side lower lobe from station 740 back to the wing box cut-out, and from the window level down to the cargo deck floor (the fracture line along stringer 38L), had peeled outwards, upwards and rearwards - separating from the rest of the fuselage at the window belt. The whole of this separated section had then continued to slide upwards and rearwards, over the fuselage, before being carried back in the slipstream and colliding with the outer leading edge of the right horizontal stabiliser, completely disrupting the outer half. A fragment of horizontal stabiliser spar cap was found embedded in the fuselage structure adjacent to the two vent valves, just below, and forward of, the L2 door [Appendix B, Figure B-22].

(v) A large, clear, imprint of semi-eliptical form was apparent on the lower right side at station 360 which had evidently been caused by the separating forward fuselage section striking the No 3 engine as it swung rearwards and to the right (confirmed by No 3 engine fan cowl damage).

Tailplane three-dimensional reconstruction

The tailplane structural design took the form of a forward and an aft torque box. The forward box was constructed from light gauge aluminium alloy sheet skins, supported by closely pitched, light gauge nose ribs but without lateral stringers. The aft torque box incorporated heavy gauge skin/stringer panels with more widely spaced ribs. The front spar web was of light gauge material. Leading edge impacts inflicted by debris would therefore have had the capacity to reduce the tailplane's structural integrity by passing through the light gauge skins and spar web into the interior of the aft torque box, damaging the shear connection between top and bottom skins in the process and thereby both removing the bending strength of the box and opening up the weakened structure to the direct effects of the airflow.

Examination of the rebuilt tailplane structure at AAIB Farnborough left little doubt that it had been destroyed by debris striking its leading edges. In addition, the presence on the skins of smear marks indicated that some unidentified soft debris had contacted those surfaces whilst moving with both longitudinal and lateral velocity components relative to the aircraft.

The reconstructed left tailplane [Appendix B, Figure B-23] showed evidence that disruption of the inboard leading edge, followed respectively by the forward torque box, front spar web and main torque box, occurred as a result of frontal impact by the base of a baggage container. Further outboard, a compact object appeared to have struck the underside of the leading edge and penetrated to the aft torque box. In both cases, the loss of the shear web of the front spar appeared to have permitted local bending failure of the remaining main torque box structure in a tip downwards sense, consistent with the normal load direction. For both events to have occured it would be reasonable to assume that the outboard damage preceded that occurring inboard.

The right tailplane exhibited massive leading edge impact damage on the outboard portion which also appeared to have progressed to disruption of the aft torsion box. A fragment of right tailplane spar cap was found embedded in the fuselage structure adjacent to the two vent valves, just below, and forward of, the L2 door and it is clear that this area of forward left fuselage had travelled over the top of the aircraft and contributed to the destruction of the outboard right tailplane.

Examination of engines

All four engines had struck the ground in Lockerbie with considerable velocity and therefore sustained major damage, in particular to most of the fan blades. The No 3 engine had fallen 1,100 metres north of the other three engines, striking the ground on its rear face, penetrating a road surface and coming to rest without any further change of orientation i.e. with the front face remaining uppermost. The intake area contained a number of loose items originating from within the cabin or baggage hold. It was not possible initially to determine whether any of the general damage to any of the engine fans or the ingestion noted in No 3 engine intake occurred whilst the relevant engines were delivering power or at a later stage.

Numbers 1, 2 and 3 engines were taken to British Airways Engine Overhaul Limited for detailed examination under AAIB supervision in conjunction with a specialist from the Pratt and Whitney Engine Company. During this examination the following points were noted:

(i)   No 2 engine (situated closest to the site of the explosion) had evidence of blade "shingling" in the area of the shrouds consistent with the results of major airflow disturbance whilst delivering power. (This effect is produced when random bending and torsional deflection occurs, permitting the mid-span shrouds to disengage and repeatedly strike the adjacent aerofoil surfaces of the blades). The interior of the air intake contained paint smears and other evidence suggesting the passage of items of debris. One such item of significance was a clear indentation produced by a length of cable of diameter and strand size similar to that typically attached to the closure curtains on the baggage containers.

(ii)   No 3 engine, identified on site as containing ingested debris from within the aircraft, nonetheless had no evidence of the type of shingling seen on the blades of No 2 engine. Such evidence is usually unmistakable and its absence is a clear indication that No 3 engine did not suffer a major intake airflow disturbance whilst delivering significant power. The intake structure was found to have been crushed longitudinally by an impact on the front face although, as stated earlier, it had struck the ground on its rear face whilst falling vertically.

(iii)   All 3 engines had evidence of blade tip rubs on the fan cases having a combination of circumference and depth greater than hitherto seen on any investigation witnessed on Boeing 747 aircraft by the Pratt and Whitney specialists. Subsequent examination of No 4 engine confirmed that it had a similar deep, large circumference tip rub. These tip-rubs on the four engines were centred at slightly different clock positions around their respective fan cases.

The Pratt and Whitney specialists supplied information which was used to interpret the evidence found on the blades and fan cases including details of engine dynamic behaviour necessary to produce the tip rub evidence. This indicated that the depth and circumference of tip rubs noted would have required a marked nose down change of aircraft pitch attitude combined with a roll rate to the left.

Pratt and Whitney also advised that:

(i)   Airflow disruption such as that presumed to have caused the shingling observed on No 2 engine fan blades was almost invariably the result of damage to the fan blade aerofoils, resulting from ingestion or blade failure.

(ii)   Tip rubs of a depth and circumference noted on all four engines could be expected to reduce the fan rotational energy on each to a negligible value within approximately 5 seconds.

(iii)   Airflow disruption sufficient to cause the extent of shingling noted on the fan blades of No 2 engine would also reduce the rotational fan energy to a negligible value within approximately 5 seconds.

CHAPTER 3

OTHER INFORMATION

Medical and pathological information

The results of the post mortem examination of the victims indicated that the majority had experienced severe multiple injuries at different stages, consistent with the in-flight disintegration of the aircraft and ground impact. There was no pathological indication of an in-flight fire and no evidence that any of the victims had been injured by shrapnel from the explosion. There was also no evidence which unequivocally indicated that passengers or cabin crew had been killed or injured by the effects of a blast. Although it is probable that those passengers seated in the immediate vicinity of the explosion would have suffered some injury as a result of blast, this would have been of a secondary or tertiary nature.

Of the casualties from the aircraft, the majority were found in areas which indicated that they had been thrown from the fuselage during the disintegration. Although the pattern of distribution of bodies on the ground was not clear cut there was some correlation with seat allocation which suggested that the forward part of the aircraft had broken away from the rear early in the disintegration process. The bodies of 10 passengers were not recovered and of these, 8 had been allocated seats in rows 23 to 28 positioned over the wing at the front of the economy section. The fragmented remains of

13 passengers who had been allocated seats around the eight missing persons were found in or near the crater formed by the wing. Whilst there is no unequivocal proof that the missing people suffered the same fate, it would seem from the pattern that the missing passengers remained attached to the wing structure until impact.

Fire

Of the several large pieces of aircraft wreckage which fell in the town of Lockerbie, one was seen to have the appearance of a ball of fire with a trail of flame. Its final path indicated that this was the No 3 engine, which embedded itself in a road in the north-east part of the town. A small post impact fire posed no hazard to adjacent property and was later extinguished with water from a hosereel. The three remaining engines landed in the Netherplace area of the town. One severed a water main and the other two, although initially on fire, were no risk to persons or property and the fires were soon extinguished.

A large, dark, delta shaped object was seen to fall at about the same time in the Sherwood area of the town. It was not on fire while in the air, however, a fireball several hundred feet across followed the impact. It was of relatively short duration and large amounts of debris were thrown into the air, the lighter particles being carried several miles downwind, while larger pieces of burning debris caused further fires, including a major one at the Townfoot Garage, up to 350 metres from the source. It was determined that the major part of both wings, which included the aircraft fuel tanks, had formed the crater. A gas main had also been ruptured during the impact.

At 19.04 hrs the Dumfries Fire Brigade Control received a call from a member of the public which indicated that there had been a "huge boiler explosion" at Westacres, Lockerbie, however, subsequent calls soon made it clear that it was an aircraft which had crashed. At 19.07 hrs the first appliances were mobile and at 1910 hrs one was in attendance in the Rosebank area. Multiple fires were identified and it soon became apparent that a major disaster had occurred in the town and the Fire Brigade Major Incident Plan was implemented. During the initial phase 15 pumping appliances from various brigades were deployed but this number was ultimately increased to 20.

At 22.09 hrs the Firemaster made an assessment of the situation. He reported that there was a series of fires over an area of the town centre extending 1 Y4 by Y2 mile. The main concentration of the fire was in the southwest of the town around

Sherwood Park and Sherwood Crescent. Appliances were in attendance at other fires in the town, particularly in Park Place and Rosebank Crescent. Water and electricity supplies were interrupted and water had to be brought into the town.

By 02.22 hrs on 22 December, all main seats of fire had been extinguished and the firemen were involved in turning over and damping down. At 04.42 hrs small fires were still occurring but had been confined to the Sherwood Crescent area.

Survival aspects

Survivability

The accident was not survivable.

Emergency services

A chronology of initial responses by the emergency services is listed below:

Time	Event
19.03 hrs	Radio message from Police patrol in Lockerbie to Dumfries andGalloway Constabulary reporting an aircraft crash at Lockerbie.
19.04 hrs	Emergency call to Dumfries and Galloway Fire Brigade.

19.37 hrs	First ambulances leave for Dumfries and Galloway Royal Infinnary with injured town residents. (2- serious; 3- minor)
19.40 hrs	Sherwood Park and Sherwood Crescent residents evacuated to Lockerbie Town Hall.
20.25 hrs	Nose section of N739PA discovered at Tundergarth (approximately 4 km east of Lockerbie).

During the next few days a major emergency operation was mounted using the guidelines of the Dumfries and Galloway Regional Peacetime Emergency Plan. The Dumfries and Galloway Constabulary was reinforced by contingents from Strathclyde and Lothian & Borders Constabularies. Resources from I-1M Forces were made available and this support was subsequently authorised by the Ministry of Defence as Military Aid to the Civil Power. It included the provision of military personnel and a number of helicopters used mainly in the search for and recovery of aircraft wreckage. It was apparent at an early stage that there were no survivors from the aircraft and the search and recovery of bodies was mainly a Police task with military assistance.

Many other agencies were involved in the provision of welfare and support services for the residents of Lockerbie, relatives of the aircraft's occupants and personnel involved in the emergency operation.

Tests and research

An explosive detonation within a fuselage, in reasonably close proximity to the skin, will produce a high intensity spherically propagating shock wave which will expand outwards from the centre of detonation. On reaching the inner surface of the fuselage skin, energy will partially be absorbed in shattering, deforming and accelerating the skin and stringer material in its path. Much of the remaining energy will be transmitted, as a shock wave, through the skin and into the atmosphere but a significant amount of energy will be returned as a reflected shock wave, which will travel back into the fuselage interior where it will interact with the incident shock to produce Mach stem shocks - re-combination shock waves which can have pressures and velocities of propagation greater than the incident shock.

The Mach stem phenomenon is significant because it gives rise (for relatively small charge sizes) to a geometric limitation on the area of skin material which the incident shock wave can shatter, irrespective of charge size, thus providing a means of calculating the standoff distance of the explosive charge from the fuselage skin. Calculations suggest that a charge standoff distance of aproximately 25 inches would result in a shattered region approximately 18 to 20 inches in diameter, comparable to the size of the shattered region evident in the wreckage. This aspect is covered in greater detail in [Appendix G[.

Additional information

Recorded radar information

Recorded radar information on the aircraft was available from from 4 radar sites. Initial analysis consisted of viewing the recorded information as it was shown to the controller on the radar screen from which it was clear that the flight had progressed in a normal manner until secondary surveillance radar (SSR) was lost.

The detailed analysis of the radar information concentrated on the break-up of the aircraft. The Royal Signals and Radar Establishment (RSRE) corrected the radar returns for fixed errors and converted the SSR returns to latitude and longitude so that an accurate time and position for the aircraft could be determined. The last secondary return from the aircraft was recorded at 19.02:46.9 hrs, identifying N739PA at Flight Level 310, and at the next radar return there is no SSR data, only 4 primary returns. It was concluded that the aircraft was, by this time, no longer a single return and, considering the approximately 1 nautical mile spread of returns across track, that items had been ejected at high speed probably to both right and left of the aircraft.

Each rotation of the radar head thereafter showed the number of returns increasing, with those first identified across track having slowed down very quickly and followed a track along the prevailing wind line. The radar evidence then indicated that a further break-up of the aircraft had occurred and formed a parallel wreckage trail to the north of the first. From the absence of any returns travelling along track it was concluded that the main wreckage was travelling almost vertically downwards for much of the time.

A detailed analysis of the recorded radar information, together with the radar, ATC and seismic recordings is contained in Appendix C.

Seismic data

The British Geological Survey has a number of seismic monitoring stations in Southern Scotland. Stations close to Lockerbie recorded a seismic event measuring 1.6 on the Richter scale and, with appropriate corrections for the times of the waves to reach the sensors, it was established that this occurred at 19.03:36.5 hrs ±1 second. A further check was made by triangulation techniques from the information recorded by the various sensors.

An analysis of the seismic recording, together with the radar, ATC and radar information is contained in Appendix C.

Trajectory analysis

A detailed trajectory analysis was carried out by Cranfield Institute of Technology in an effort to provide a sequence for the aircraft disintegration. This analysis comprised several separate processes, including individual trajectory calculations for a limited number of key items of wreckage and mathematical modelling of trajectory paths adopted by a series of hypothetical items of wreckage encompassing the drag/weight spectrum of the actual wreckage.

The work carried out at Cranfield enabled the reasons for the two separate trails to be established. The narrow northern trail was shown to be created by debris released from the aircraft in a vertical dive between 19,000 and 9,000 feet overhead Lockerbie. The southern trail, longer and straight for most of its length, appeared to have been created by wreckage released during the initial disintegration at altitude whilst the aircraft was in level flight. Those items falling closest to Lockerbie would have been those with higher density which would travel a significant distance along track before losing all along-track velocity, whilst only drifting a small distance downwind, owing to the high speed of their descent. The most westerly items thus showed the greatest such effect. The southern trail therefore had curved boundaries at its western end with the curvature becoming progressively less to the east until the wreckage essentially fell in a straight band. Thus wreckage in the southern trail positioned well to the east could be assumed to have retained negligible velocity along aircraft track after separation and the along-track distribution could be used to establish an approximate sequence of initial disintegration.

The analysis calculated impact speeds of 120 kts for the nose section weighing approximately 17,500 lb and 260 kts for the engines and pylons which each weighed about 13,500 lb. Based on the best available data at the time, the analysis showed that the wing (approximately 100,000 lb of structure containing an estimated 200,000 lb of fuel) could have impacted at a speed, in theory, as high as 650 kts if it had 'flown' in a streamlined attitude such that the drag coefficient was minimal. However, because small variations of wing incidence (and various amounts of attached fuselage) could have resulted in significant increases in drag coefficient, the analysis also recognized that the final impact speed of the wing could have been lower.

Space debris re-entry

Four items of space debris were known to have re-entered the Earth's atmosphere on 21 December 1988. Three of these items were fragments of debris which would not have survived re-entry, although their burn up in the upper atmosphere might have been visible from the Earth's surface. The fourth item landed in the USSR at 09.50 hrs UTC.

ANALYSIS

CHAPTER 4

ANALYSIS

Introduction

The airport security and criminal aspects of the destruction of Boeing 747 registration N739PA near Lockerbie on 21 December 1988 are the subjects of a separate investigation and are not covered in this report. This analysis discusses the technical aspects of the disintegration of the aircraft and considers possible ways of mitigating the effects of an explosion in the future.

Explosive destruction of the aircraft

The geographical position of the final secondary return at 19.02:46.9 hrs was calculated by RSRE to be OS Grid Reference 15257772, annotated Point A in Appendix B, Figure B-4, with an accuracy considered to be better than ±300 metres This return was received 3.1±1 seconds before the loud sound was recorded on the CVR at 19.02:50 hrs. By projecting from this position along the track of 321°(Grid) for 3.1±1 seconds at the groundspeed of 434 kts, the position of the aircraft was calculated to be OS Grid Reference 14827826, annotated Point B in Appendix B, Figure B-4, within an accuracy of ±525 metres. Based on the evidence of recorded data only, Point B therefore represents the geographical position of the aircraft at the moment the loud sound was recorded on the CVR.

The datum line was derived from a detailed analysis of the distribution of specific items of wreckage, including those exhibiting positive evidence of a detonating high performance plastic explosive. The scatter of these items about the datum line may have been due partly to velocities imparted by the force of the detonating explosive and partly by the difficulty experienced in pinpointing the location of the wreckage accurately in relatively featureless terrain and poor visibility. However, the random nature of the scatter created by these two effects would have tended to counteract one another, and a major error in any one of the eleven grid references would have had little overall effect on the whole line. There is, therefore, good reason to have confidence in the validity of the datum line.

The items used to define the datum line, included those exhibiting positive evidence of a detonating high performance plastic explosive, would have been the first pieces to have been released from the aircraft. The datum line was projected westwards until it intersected the known radar track of the aircraft in order to derive the position of the aircraft along track at which the explosive items were released and therefore the position at which the IED had detonated. This position was OS grid reference 146786 and is annotated Point C in Appendix B, Figure B-4. Point C was well within the circle of accuracy (± 525 metres) of the position at which the loud noise was heard on the CVR (Point B). There can, therefore, be no doubt that the loud noise on the CVR was directly associated with the detonation of the IED and that this explosion initiated the disintegration process and directly caused the loss of the aircraft.

Flight recorders

Digital flight data recordings

A working group of the European Organisation for Civil Aviation Electronics (EUROCAE) was, during the period of the investigation, formulating new standards (Minimum Operational Performance Requirement for Flight Data Recorder Systems,

Ref:- ED55) for future generation flight recorders which would have permitted delays between parameter input and recording (buffering) of up to Y2 second. These standards are intended to form the basis of new CAA specifications for flight recorders and may be adopted worldwide.

The analysis of the recording from the DFDR fitted to N739PA, which is detailed in Appendix C, showed that the recorded data simply stopped. Following careful examination and correlation of the various sources of recorded information, it was concluded that this occurred because the electrical power supply to the recorder had been interrupted at 19.02:50 hrs ±1 second. Only 17 bits of data were not recoverable (less that 23 milliseconds) and it was not possible to establish with any certainty if this data was from the accident flight or was old data from a previous recording.

The analysis of the final data recorded on the DFDR was possible because the system did not buffer the incoming data. Some existing recorders use a process whereby data is stored temporarily in a memory device (buffer) before recording. The data within this buffer is lost when power is removed from the recorder and in currently designed recorders this may mean that up to 1.2 seconds of final data contained within the buffer is lost. Due to the necessary processing of the signals prior to input to the recorder, additional delays of up to 300 milliseconds may be introduced. If the accident had occurred when the aircraft was over the sea, it is very probable that the relatively few small items of structure, luggage and clothing showing positive evidence of the detonation of an explosive device would not have been recovered. However, as flight recorders are fitted with underwater location beacons, there is a high probability that they would have been located and recovered. In such an event the final milliseconds of data contained on the DFDR could be vital to the successful determination of the cause of an accident whether due to an explosive device or other catastrophic failure. Whilst it may not be possible to reduce some of the delays external to the recorder, it is possible to reduce any data loss due to buffering of data within the data acquisition unit.

It is, therefore, recommended that manufacturers of existing recorders which use buffering techniques give consideration to making the buffers non-volatile, and hence recoverable after power loss. Although the recommendation on this aspect, made to the EUROCAE working group during the investigation, was incorporated into ED55, it is also recommended that Airworthiness Authorities re-consider the concept of allowing buffered data to be stored in a volatile memory.

Cockpit voice recorders

The analysis of the cockpit voice recording, which is detailed in Appendix C, concluded that there were valid signals available to the CVR when it stopped at 19.02:50 hrs ±1 second because the power supply to the recorder was interrupted. It is not clear if the sound at the end of the recording is the result of the explosion or is from the break-up of the aircraft structure. The short period between the beginning of the event and the loss of electrical power suggests that the latter is more likely to be the case. In order to respond to events that result in the almost immediate loss of the aircraft's electrical power supply it was therefore recommended during the investigation that the regulatory authorities consider requiring CVR systems to contain a short duration (i.e. no greater than 1 minute) back-up power supply.

Detection of explosive occurrences

In the aftermath of the Air India Boeing 747 accident (AI 182) in the North Atlantic on 23 June 1985, RARDE were asked informally by AAIB to examine means of differentiating, by recording violent cabin pressure pulses, between the detonation of an explosive device within the cabin (positive pulse) and a catastrophic structural failure (negative pulse). Following the Lockerbie disaster it was considered that this work should be raised to a formal research project. Therefore, in February 1989, it was recommended that the Department of Transport fund a study to devise methods of recording violent positive and negative pressure pulses, utilising the aircraft's flight recorder systems. This recommendation was accepted.

Preliminary results from the trials indicate that, if a suitable sensor can be developed, its output will need to be recorded in real time and therefore it may require wiring to the CVR installation. This will further strengthen the requirement for battery back up of the CVR electrical power supply

IED position within the aircraft

From the detailed examination of the reconstructed luggage containers, discussed in Appendix F, it was evident that the IED had been located within a metal container (serial number AVE 4041 PA), near its aft outboard quarter as shown in Appendix F, Figure F-13. It was also clear that the container was loaded in position 14L of the forward hold which placed the explosive charge approximately 25 inches inboard from the fuselage skin at frame 700. There was no evidence to indicate that there was more than one explosive charge.

Engine evidence

To produce the fan blade tip rub damage noted on all engines by means of airflow inclined to the axes of the nacelles would have required a marked nose down change of aircraft pitch attitude combined with a roll rate to the left while all of the engines were attached to the wing.The shingling damage noted on the fan blades of No 2 engine can only be attributed to airflow disturbance caused by ingestion related fan blade damage occurring when substantial power was being delivered. This is readily explained by the fact that No 2 engine intake is positioned some 27 feet aft and 30 feet outboard of the site of the explosion and that the interior of the intake exhibited a number of prominent paint smears and general foreign object damage. This damage included evidence of a strike by a cable similar to that forming part of the closure curtain of a typical baggage container. It is inconceivable that an independent blade failure could have occurred in the short time frame of this event. By similar reasoning, the absence of such shingling damage on blades of No 3 engine was a reliable indication that it suffered no ingestion until well into the accident sequence. The combination of the position of the explosive device and the forward speed of the aircraft was such that significant sized debris resulting from the explosion would have been available to be ingested by No 2 engine within milliseconds of the explosion. In view of the fact that the tip rub damage observed on the fan case of No 2 engine is of similar magnitude to that observed on the other three engines it is reasonable to deduce that a manoeuvre of the aircraft occurred before most of the energy of the No 2 engine fan was lost due to the effect of ingestion (seen only in this engine). Since this shingling effect could only readily be produced as a by-product of ingestion whilst delivering considerable power, it is reasonable to assume that this was also occurring before loss of major fan energy due to tip rubbing took place. Hence both phenomena must have been occurring simultaneously, or nearly so, to produce the effects observed and must have occupied a time frame of substantially less than 5 seconds. The onset of this time period would have been the time at which debris from the explosion first inflicted damage to fan blades in No 3 engine and, since the fan is only approximately 40 feet from the location of the explosive device, this would have been an insignificant time interval after the explosion.

It was therefore concluded from this evidence that the wing with all of the engines attached had achieved a marked nose down and left roll attitude change well within 5 seconds of the explosion.

Detachment of forward fuselage

Examination of the three major structural elements either side of the region of station 800 on the right side of the fuselage makes it clear that to produce the curvature of the window belt and peeling of the riveted joint at the R2 door aperture requires the door pillar to be securely in position and able to react longitudinal and lateral loads. This in turn requires the large section of fuselage on the right side between stations 760 and 1000 (incorporating the right half of the floor) to be in position in order to locate the lower end of the door pillar. Thus both these sections must have been in position until the section from station 560 to 800 (right side) had completed its deflection to the right and peeled from the door pillar. Separation of the forward fuselage must thus have been complete by the time all three items mentioned above had fallen free.

Speed of initial disintegration

The distribution of wreckage in the bands between the datum line and the 250, 300, 600 and 900 metre lines was examined in detail. The positions of these items of structure on the aircraft are shown in Appendix B, Figures B-10 to B-13. It should be noted that the position on the ground of these items, although separated by small distances when measured in a direction along aircraft track, were distributed over large distances when measured along the wreckage trail. All were recovered from positions far enough to the east to be in that part of the southern trail which was sufficiently close, theoretically, to a straight line for any curvature effect to be neglected. The wreckage found in each of the bands enabled an approximate sequence of break-up to be established. It was clear that as the distance travelled from the datum line increased, items of wreckage further from the station of the IED were encountered. The items shown on the diagram as falling on the 250 metre band also include those fragments of lower forward fuselage skin having evidence of explosive damage and presumed to have separated as a direct result of the blast. However, a few portions of the upper forward fuselage were also found within the 250 metre band, suggesting that these items had also separated as a result of the blast.

By the time the 300 metre line was reached much of the structure from the right side in the region of the explosive device had been shed. This included the area of window belt, referred to in paragraph 2.6 above, which gave clear indications that the forward structure had detached to the right and finally peeled away at station 800. It also included the areas of adjacent structure immediately to the rear of station 800 about which the forward structure would have had to pivot. By the time the 600 metre line was reached, there was clearly insufficient structure left to connect the forward fuselage with the remainder of the aircraft. Wreckage between the 600 and 900 metre lines consisted of structure still further from the site of the IED.

There is evidence that a manoeuvre occurred at the time of the explosion which would have produced a significant change of the aircraft's flight path, however, it is considered that the change in the horizontal velocity component in the first few seconds would not have been great. The original groundspeed of the aircraft was therefore used in conjunction with the distribution of wreckage in the successive bands to establish an approximate time sequence of break-up of the forward fuselage. Assuming the original ground speed of 434 Kts, the elapsed flight times from the datum to each of the parellel lines were calculated to be:

Distance (metres)	250	300	600	900
Time (seconds	1.1	1.3	2.7	4.0

Thus, there is little doubt that separation of the forward fuselage was complete within 2 to 3 seconds of the explosion.

The separate assessment of the known grid references of tailplane and elevator wreckage in the southern trail revealed that those items were evenly distributed about the 600 metre line and therefore that most of the tailplane damage occured after separation of the forward fuselage was complete.

The manoeuvre following the explosion

The engine evidence, timing and mode of disintegration of the fuselage and tailplane suggests that the latter did not sustain significant damage until the forward fuselage disintegration was well advanced and the pitch/roll manoeuvre was also well under way

Examination of the three dimensional reconstruction makes it clear that both main and upper deck floors were disrupted by the explosion. Since pitch control cables are routed through the upper deck floor beams and the roll control cables through the main deck beams, there is a strong possibility that movement of the beams under explosive forces would have applied inputs to the control cables, thus operating control surfaces in both axes.

Secondary disintegration

The distribution of fin debris between the trails suggests that disintegration of the fin began shortly before the vertical descent was established. No single mode of failure was identified and the debris which had struck the leading edge had not caused major disruption. The considerable fragmentation of the thick panels of the aft torque box was also very different from that noted on the corresponding structure of the tailplanes. It was therefore concluded that the mode of failure was probably flutter.

The finding, in the northern trail, of a slide raft wrapped around a flap track fairing suggests that at a later stage of the disintegration the rear of the aircraft must have experienced a large angle of sideslip. The loss of the fin would have made this possible and also subjected the structure to large side loads. It is possible that such side loading would have assisted the disintegration of the rear fuselage and also have caused bending failure of the pylon attachments of the remaining three engines.

Impact speed of components

The trajectory analysis carried out by Cranfield Institute of Technology calculated impact speeds of 120 kts for the nose section, and 260 kts for the engines and pylons. These values were considered to be reliable because the drag coefficients could be estimated with a reasonable degree of confidence. Based on the best available data at the time, the analysis also showed that the wing could have impacted at a speed, in theory, as high as 650 kts if it had flown in a streamlined attitude such that the drag coefficient was minimal. However, it was also recognized that relatively small changes in the angle of incidence of the wing would have produced a significant increase in drag with a consequent reduction in impact speed. Refinement of timing information and radar data subsequent to the Cranfield analysis has enabled a revised estimate to be made of the mean speed of the wing during the descent

The engine evidence indicated that there had been a large nose down attitude change of the aircraft early in the event. The Cranfield analysis also showed that the rear fuselage had disintegrated while essentially in a vertical descent between 19,000 and 9,000 feet over Lockerbie. Assuming that, following the explosion, the wing followed a straight line descending flight profile from 31,000 feet to 19,000 feet directly overhead Lockerbie and then descended vertically until impact, the wing would have travelled the minimum distance practicable. The ground distance between the geographical position at which the disintegration started (Figure B-4, Point B) and the crater made by the wing impact was 2997 ±525 metres (9833 ±1722 feet). The time interval between the explosion and the wing impact was established in Appendix C as 46.5 ±2 seconds. Based on the above times and distances the mean linear speed achieved by the wing would have been about 440 kts.

The impact location of Nos 1, 2, and 4 engines closely grouped in Lockerbie was consistent with their nearly vertical fall from a point above the town. If they had separated at about 19,000 feet and the wing had then flown as much as one mile away from the overhead position before tracking back to impact, the total flight path length of the wing would not have required it to have achieved a mean linear speed in excess of 500 kts.

Any speculation that the flight path of the wing could have been longer would have required it to have undergone manoeuvres at high speed in order to arrive at the 19,000 feet point. The manoeuvres involved would almost certainly have resulted in failure of the primary wing structure which, from distribution of wing debris, clearly did not occur. Alternatively the wing could have travelled more than one mile from Lockerbie after reaching the 19,000 feet point, but this was considered unlikely. It is therefore concluded that the mean speed of the wing during the descent was in the region of 440 to 500 kts.

Sequence of disintegration

Analysis of wreckage in each of the bands, taken in conjunction with the engine evidence and the three-dimensional reconstruction, suggests the following sequence of disintegration:

(i)   The initial explosion triggered a sequence of events which effectively destroyed the structural integrity of the forward fuselage. Little more then remained between stations 560 and 760 (approximately) than the window belts and the cabin sidewall structure imediately above and below the windows, although much of the cargo-hold floor structure appears to have remained briefly attached to the aircraft. [Appendix **B,** Figure B-24]

(ii)   The main portion of the aircraft simultaneously entered a manoeuvre involving a marked nose down and left roll attitude change, probably as a result of inputs applied to the flying control cables by movement of structure.

(iii)   Failure of the left window belt then occured, probably in the region of station 710, as a result of torsional and bending loads on the fuselage imparted by the manoeuvre (i.e. the movement of the forward fuselage relative to the remainder of the aircraft was an initial twisting motion to the right, accompanied by a nose up pitching deflection).

(iv)   The forward fuselage deflected to the right, pivoting about the starboard window belt, and then peeled away from the structure at station 800. During this process the lower nose section struck the No 3 engine intake causing the engine to detach from its pylon. This fuselage separation was apparently complete within 3 seconds of the explosion.

(v)   Structure and contents of the forward fuselage struck the tail surfaces contributing to the destruction of the outboard starboard tailplane and causing substantial damage to the port unit. This damage occurred approximately 600 metres track distance after the explosion and therefore appears to have happened after the fuselage separation was complete.

(vi)   Fuselage structure continued to break away from the aircraft and the separated forward fuselage section as they descended.

(vii)   The aircraft maintained a steepening descent path until it reached the vertical in the region of 19,000 feet approximately over the final impact point. Shortly before it did so the tail fin began to disintegrate.

(viii) The mode of failure of the fin is not clear, however, flutter of its structure is suspected.

(ix)   Once established in the vertical dive, the fin torque box continued to disintegrate, possibly permitting the remainder of the aircraft to yaw sufficiently to cause side load separation of Nos 1, 2 and 4 engines, complete with their pylons.

(x)   Break-up of the rear fuselage occurred during the vertical descent, possibly as a result of loads induced by the yaw, leaving a section of cabin floor and baggage hold from approximately stations 1241 to 1920, together with 3 landing gear units, to fall into housing at Rosebank Terrace.

(xi)   The main wing structure struck the ground with a high yaw angle at Sherwood Crescent.

Explosive mechanisms and the structural disintegration

The fracture and damage pattern analysis was mainly of an interpretive nature involving interlocking pieces of subtle evidence such as paint smears, fracture and rivet failure characteristics, and other complex features. In the interests of brevity, this analysis will not discuss the detailed interpretation of individual fractures or damage features. Instead, the broader 'damage picture' which emerged from the detailed work will be discussed in the context of the explosive mechanisms which might have produced the damage, with a view to identifying those features of greatest significance.

It is important to keep in mind that whilst the processes involved are considered and discussed separately, the timescales associated with shock wave propagation and the high velocity gas flows are very short compared with the structural response timescales. Consequently, material which was shattered or broken by the explosive forces would have remained in place for a sufficiently long time that the structure can be considered to have been intact throughout much of the period that these explosive propagation phenomena were taking place.

Shock wave propagation

The direct effect of the explosive detonation within the container was to produce a high intensity spherically propagating shock wave which expanded from the centre of detonation close to the side of the container, shattering part of the side and base of the container as it passed through into the gap between the container and the fuselage skin. In breaking out of the container, some internal reflection and Mach stem interaction would have occurred, but this would have been limited by the absorptive effect of the baggage inboard, above, and forward of the charge. The force of the explosion breaking out of the container would therefore have been directed downwards and rearwards.

The heavy container base was distorted and torn downwards, causing buckling of the adjoining section of frame 700, and the container sides were blasted through and torn, particularly in the aft lower corner. Some of the material in the direct path of the explosive pressure front was reduced to shrapnel sized pieces which were rapidly accelerated outwards behind the primary shock front. Because of the overhang of the container's sloping side, fragments from both the device itself and the container wall impacted the projecting external flange of the container base edge member, producing micro cratering and sooting. Metallurgical examination of the internal surfaces of these craters identified areas of melting and other features which were consistent only with the impact of very high energy particles produced by an explosion at close quarters. Analysis of material on the crater surfaces confirmed the presence of several elements and compounds foreign to the composition of the edge member, including material consistent with the composition of the sheet aluminium forming the sloping face of the container.

On reaching the inner surface of the fuselage skin, the incident shock wave energy would partially have been absorbed in shattering, deforming and accelerating the skin and stringer material in its path. Much of its energy would have been transmitted, as a shock wave, through the skin and into the atmosphere [Appendix B, Figure B-25], but a significant amount of energy would have been returned as a reflected shock wave, back into the cavity between the container and the fuselage skin where Mach stem shock waves would have been formed. Evidence of rapid shattering was found in a region approximately bounded by frames 700 & 720 and stringers 38L & 40L, together with the lap joint at 39L.

The shattered fuselage skin would have taken a significant time to move, relative to the timescales associated with the primary shock wave propagation. Clear evidence of soot and small impact craters were apparent on the internal surfaces of all fragments of container and structure from the shatter zone, confirming that the this material had not had time to move before it was hit by the cloud of shrapnel, unburnt explosive residues and sooty combustion products generated at the seat of the explosion.

Following immediately behind the primary shock wave, a secondary high pressure wave - partly caused by reflections off the baggage behind the explosive material but mainly by the general pressure rise caused by the chemical conversion of solid explosive material to high temperature gas - emerged from the container. The effect of this second pressure front, which would have been more sustained and spread over a much larger area, was to cause the fuselage skin to stretch and blister outwards before bursting and petalling back in a star-burst pattern, with rapidly running tear fractures propagating away from a focus at the shatter zone. The release of stored energy as the skin ruptured, combined with the outflow of high pressure gas through the aperture, produced a characteristic curling of the skin 'petals' - even against the slipstream. For the most part, the skins which petalled back in this manner were torn from the frames and stringers, but the frames and stringers themselves were also fractured and became separated from the rest of the structure, producing a very large jagged hole some 5 feet longitudinally by 17 feet circumferentially (upwards to a region just below the window belt and downwards virtually to the centre line).

From this large jagged hole, three of the fractures continued to propagate away from the hole instead of terminating at the boundary. One fracture propagated longitudinally rearwards as far as the wing cut-out and another forwards to station 480, creating a continuous longitudinal fracture some 43 feet in length. A third fracture propagated circumferentially downwards along frame 740, under the belly, and up the right side of the fuselage almost as far as the window belt - a distance of approximately 23 feet.

These extended fractures all involved tearing or related failure modes, sometimes exploiting rivet lines and tearing from rivet hole to rivet hole, in other areas tearing along the full skin section adjacent to rivet lines, but separate from them. Although the fractures had, in part, followed lap joints, the actual failure modes indicated that the joints themselves were not inherently weak, either as design features or in respect of corrosion or the conditions of the joints on this particular aircraft.

Note: The cold bond process carried out at manufacture on the lap joints had areas of disbonding prior to the accident. This disbonding is a known feature of early Boeing 747 aircraft which, by itself, does not detract from the structural integrity of the hull. The cold bond adhesive was used to improve the distribution of shear load across the joint, thus reducing shear transfer via the fasteners and improving the resistance of the joint to fatigue damage; the fasteners were designed to carry the full static loading requirements of the joint without any contribution from the adhesive. Thus, the loss of the cold bond integrity would only have been significant if it had resulted in the growth of fatigue cracks, or corrosion induced weaknesses, which had then been exploited by the explosive forces. No evidence of fatigue cracking was found in the bonded joints. Inter-surface corrosion was present on most lap joints but only one very small region of corrosion had resulted in significant material thinning; this was remote from the critical region and had not played any part in the break–up.

The cracks propagating upwards as part of the petalling process did not extend beyond the window line. The wreckage evidence suggests that the vertical fractures merged, effectively closing off the fracture path to produce a relatively clean bounding edge to the upper section of the otherwise jagged hole produced by the petalling process. There are at least two probable reasons for this. Firstly the petalling fractures above the shattered zone did not diverge, as they had tended to do elsewhere. Instead, it appears that a large skin panel separated and peeled upwards very rapidly producing tears at each side which ran upwards following almost parallel paths. However, there are indications that by the time the fractures had run several feet, the velocity of fracture had slowed sufficiently to allow the free (forward) edge of the skin panel to overtake the fracture fronts, as it flexed upwards, and forcibly strike the fuselage skin above, producing clear witness marks on both items. Such a tearing process, in which an approximately rectangular flap of skin is pulled upwards away from the main skin panel, is likely to result in the fractures merging. Secondly, this merging tendency would have been reinforced in this particular instance by the stiff window belt ahead of the fractures, which would have tended to turn the fractures towards the horizontal.

It appears that the presence of this initial ('clean') hole, together with the stiff window belt above, encouraged other more slowly running tears to break into it, rather than propagating outwards away from the main hole.

Critical crack considerations

The three very large tears extending beyond the boundary of the petalled region resulted in a critical reduction of fuselage structural integrity.

Calculations were carried out at the Royal Aerospace Establishment to determine whether these fractures, growing outwards from the boundary of the petalled hole, could have occurred purely as a result of normal differential pressure loading of the fuselage, or whether explosive forces were required in addition to the pressurisation loads.

Preliminary calculations of critical crack dimensions for a fuselage skin punctured by a 20 by 20 inches jagged hole indicated that unstable crack growth would not have occurred unless the skin stress had been substantially greater than the stress level due to normal pressurisation loads alone. It was therefore clear that explosive overpressure must have produced the gross enlargement of the initially small shattered hole in the hull. Furthermore, it was apparent from the degree of curling and petalling of the skin panels within the star-burst region that this overpressure had been relatively long term, compared with the shock wave overpressure which had produced the shatter zone. A more refined analysis of critical crack growth parameters was therefore carried out in which it was assumed that the long term explosive overpressure was produced by the chemical conversion of solid explosive material into high temperature gas.

An outline of the fracture propagation analysis is given at Appendix D. This analysis, using theoretical fracture mechanics, showed that, after the incident shock wave had produced the shatter zone, significant explosive overpressure loads were needed to drive the star-burst fractures out to the boundary of the petalled skin zone. Thereafter, residual gas overpressure combined with fuselage pressurisation loads were sufficient to produce the two major longitudinal cracks and a single major circumferential crack, extending from the window belt down to beyond the keel centreline.

Damage to the cabin floor structure

The floor beams in the region immediately above the baggage container in which the explosive had detonated were extensively broken, displaying clear indications of overload failure due to buckling caused by localised upward loading of the floor structure.

No direct evidence of bruising was found on the top panel of the container. It therefore appears that the container did not itself impact the floor beams, but instead the floor immediately above the container was broken through as a result of explosive overpressure as gases emerged from the ruptured container and loaded the floor panels. Data on floor strengths, provided by Boeing, indicated that the cabin floor (with the CRAF modification) would fail at a uniform static differential pressure of between 3.5 and 3.9 psi (high pressure below the cabin floor), and that the floor panel to floor beam attachments would not fail before the floor beams. Whilst there is no direct evidence of the pressure loading on the floor structure immediately following detonation, there can be no doubt that in the region of station 700 it would have exceeded the ultimate failure load by a large margin.

Indirect explosive damage (damage at remote sites)

All of the damage considered in the foregoing analysis, and the mechanisms giving rise to that damage, resulted from the direct impact of explosive shock waves and/or the short-term explosive overpressure on structure close to the source of the explosion.

However, there were several regions of skin separation at sites remote from the explosion which were much more difficult to understand. These remote sites formed islands of indirect explosive damage separated from the direct damage by a sea of more generalised structural failure characterised by the progressive aerodynamic break-up of the weakened forward fuselage. All of these remote damage sites were consistent with the impact of very localised pressure impulses on the internal surfaces of the hull -effectively high energy 'pressure blows' against the inner surfaces produced by explosive shock waves and/or high pressure gas flows travelling through the interior spaces of the hull.

The propagation of explosive shock waves and supersonic gas flows within multiple, interlinking, cavities having indeterminate energy absorption and reflection properties, and ill-defined structural response, is extremely complex.

Work has been initiated in an attempt to produce a three-dimensional computer analysis of the shock wave and supersonic flow propagation inside the fuselage, but full theoretical analysis is beyond present resources.

Because of the complexity of the problem, the following analysis will be restricted to a qualitative consideration of the processes which were likely to have taken place. Whilst such an approach is necessarily limited, it has identified a number of propagation mechanisms which appear to have been of fundamental importance to the break-up of Flight PA103, and which are likely to be critical in any future incident involving the detonation of high explosive inside an aircraft hull.

Shock wave propagation through internal cavities

When Mach stem shocks are produced not only are the shock pressures very high but they propagate at very high velocity parallel to the reflecting surface. In the context of the lower fuselage structure in the region of Mach stem formation, it can readily be seen that the Mach stem will be perfectly orientated to enter the narrow cavity formed between the outer skin and the cargo liner/containers, bounded by the fuselage frames [Appendix B, Figure B-25]. This cavity enables the Mach stem shock wave to propagate, without causing damage to the walls (due to the relatively low pressure where the Mach stem sweeps their surface), and reach regions of the fuselage remote from the source of the explosion. Furthermore, energy losses in the cavity are likely to be less than would occur in the 'free' propagation case, resulting in the efficient transmission of explosive energy. The cavity would tend to act like a 'shock tube', used for high speed aerodynamic research, confining the shock wave and keeping it running along the cavity axis, with losses being limited to kinetic heating due to friction at the walls.

Before proceeding further and considering how the shock waves might have propagated through this network of cavities, it should be pointed out that the timescale associated with the propagation of the shock waves is very short compared with the timescale associated with physical movement and separation of skin and structure fractured or damaged by the shock. Therefore, for the purpose of assessing the shock propagation through the cavities, the explosive damage to the hull can be ignored and the structure regarded as being intact. A further simplification can usefully be made by considering the structure to be rigid. This assumption would, if the analysis were quantitative, result in over-estimations of the shock strengths. However, for the purposes of a purely qualitative assessment, the assumption should be valid, in that the general trends of behaviour should not be materially altered.

It has already been argued that the shock wave emerging from the container was, in part, reflected back off the inner surface of the fuselage skin, forming a Mach stem shock wave which would then have tended to travel into the semi-circular lower lobe cavity. The Mach stem waves would have propagated away through this cavity in two directions:

(i)   under the belly, between the frames [Appendix B, Figure B-3, detail A], and

(ii)   up the left side, expanding into the cavity formed by the longitudinal manifold chamber where it joins the lower lobe cavity.

As the shock waves travelled along the cavity, little attenuation or other change of characteristic was likely to have occurred until the shocks passed the entrances to other cavities, or impinged upon projections and other local changes in the cavity. A review of the literature dealing with propagation of blast waves within such cavities provides useful insights into some of the physical mechanisms involved.

As part of a research program carried out into the design of ventilation systems for blast hardened installations intended to survive the long duration blast waves following the detonation of nuclear weapons, the propagation of blast waves along the primary passages and into the side branches of ventilation ducts was studied. The research showed that 90° bends in the ducts produced very little attenuation of shock wave pressure; a series of six right angle bends produced only a 30% pressure attenuation, together with an extension of the shock duration. It is therefore evident that the attenuation of shock waves propagating through the fuselage cavities, all of which were short with hardly any right angle turns, would have been minimal.

It was also demonstrated that secondary shock waves develop within the entrance to any side branch from the main duct, produced by the interaction of the primary shock wave with the geometric changes in the duct walls at-the side-branch location. These secondary shock waves interact as they propagate into the side branch, combining together within a relatively short distance (typically 7 diameters) to produce a single, plane shock wave travelling along the duct axis. In a rigid, smooth walled structure, this mechanism produces secondary shock overpressures in the side branch of between 30% and 50% of the value of the primary shock, together with a corresponding attenuation of the primary shock wave pressure by approximately 20% to 25%.

This potential for the splitting up and re-transmission of shock wave energy within the lower hull cavities is of extreme importance in the context of this accident. Though the precise form of the interactions is too complex to predict quantitatively, it is evident that the lower hull cavities will serve to convey the overpressure efficiently to other parts of the aircraft. Furthermore, the cavities are not of serial form, i.e. they do not simply branch (and branch again) in a divergent manner, but instead form a parallel network of short cavities which reconnect with each other at many different points, principally along the crease beams. Thus, considerable scope exists for: the additive recombination of blast waves at cavity junctions; for the sustaining of the shock overpressure over a greater time period; and, for the generation of multiple shocks produced by the delay in shock propagation inherent in the different shock path (i.e. cavity) lengths.

Whilst it has not been possible to find a specific mechanism to explain the regions of localised skin separation and peel-back, they were almost certainly the result of high intensity shock overpressures produced locally in those regions as a result of the additive recombination of shock waves transmitted through the lower hull cavities. It is considered that the relatively close proximity of the left side region of damage just below floor level at station 500, [Appendix B, Figure B-19, region D] to the forward end of the cargo hold may be significant insofar as the reflections back from the forward end of the hold would have produced a local enhancement of the shock overpressure. Similarly, 'end blockage effects' produced by the cargo door frame might have been responsible for local enhancements in the area of the belly skin separation and curl-back at station 560 [Appendix B, Figure B-19 and B-20, region E].

The separation of the large section of upper fuselage skin [Appendix B, Figure B19 and B-20, detail B] was almost certainly associated with a local overpressure in the side cavities between the main deck window line and the upper deck floor, where the cavity is effectively closed off. It is considered that the most probable mechanism producing this region of impulse overpressure was a reflection from the closed end of the cavity, possibly combined with further secondary reflections from the window assembly, the whole being driven by reflective overpressures at the forward end of the longitudinal manifold cavity caused by the forward end of the cargo hold. The local overpressure inside the sidewall cavity would have been backed up by a general cabin overpressure resulting from the floor breakthrough, giving rise to an increased pressure acting on the inner face of the cabin side liner panels. This would have provided pseudo mass to the panels, effectively preventing them from moving inwards and allowing them to react the impulse pressure within the cavity, producing the region of local high pressure evidenced by the region of quilting on the skin panels [Appendix B, Figure B-19, region C].

Propagation of shock waves into the cabin

The design of the air-conditioning/depressurisation-venting systems on the Boeing 747 (and on most other commercial aircraft) is seen as a significant factor in the transmission of explosive energy, as it provides a direct connection between the main passenger cabin and the lower hull at the confluence of the lower hull cavities below the crease beam. The floor level air conditioning vents along the length of the cabin provided a series of apertures through which explosive shock waves, propagating through the sub floor cavities, would have radiated into the main cabin.

Once the shock waves entered the cabin space, the form of propagation would have been significantly different from that which occurred in the cavities in the lower hull. Again, the precise form of such radiation cannot be predicted, but it is clear that the energy would potentially have been high and there would also (potentially) have been a large number of shock waves radiating into the cabin, both from individual vents and in total, with further potential to recombine additively or to 'follow one another up' producing, in effect, sustained shock overpressures.

Within the cabin, the presence of hard, reflective, surfaces are likely to have been significant. Again, the precise way in which the shock waves interacted is vastly beyond the scope of current analytical methods and computing power, but there clearly was considerable potential for additive recombination of the many different shock waves entering at different points along the cabin and the reflected shock waves off hard surfaces in the cabin space, such as the toilet and galley compartments and overhead lockers. These recombination effects, though not understood, are known phenomena. Appendix B, Figure B-26 shows how shock waves radiating from floor level might have been reflected in such a way as produce shock loading on a localised area of the pressure hull.

Supersonic gas flows

The gas produced by the explosive would have resulted in a supersonic flow of very high pressure gas through the structural cavities, which would have followed up closely behind the shock waves. Whilst the physical mechanisms of propagation would have been different from those of the shock wave, the end result would have been similar, i.e. there would have been propagation via multiple, linked paths, with potential for additive recombination and successive pressure pulses resulting from differing path lengths. Essentially, the shock waves are likely to have delivered initial 'pressure blows' which would then have been followed up immediately by more sustained pressures resulting from the high pressure supersonic gas flows.

Potential limitation of explosive damage

Quite clearly the detonation of high explosive material anywhere on board an aircraft is potentially catastrophic and the most effective means of protecting lives is to stop such material entering the aircraft in the first place. However, it is recognised that such risks cannot be eliminated entirely and it is therefore essential that means are sought to reduce the vulnerability of commercial aircraft structures to explosive damage.

The processes which take place when an explosive detonates inside an aircraft fuselage are complex and, to a large extent, fickle in terms of the precise manner in which the processes occur. Furthermore, the potential variation in charge size, position within the hull, and the nature of the materials in the immediate vicinity of the charge (baggage etc) are such that it would be unrealistic to expect to neutralise successfully the effect of every potential explosive device likely to be placed on board an aircraft. However, whilst the problem is intractable so far as a total solution is concerned, it should be possible to limit the damage caused by an explosive device inside a baggage container on a Boeing 747 or similar aircraft to a degree which would allow the aircraft to land successfully, albeit with severe local damage and perhaps resulting in some loss of life or injuries.

In Appendix E the problem of reducing the vulnerability of commercial aircraft to explosive damage is discussed, both in general terms and in the context of aircraft of similar size and form to the Boeing 747. In that discussion, those damage mechanisms which appear to have contributed to the catastrophic structural failure of Flight PA103 are identified and possible ways of reducing their damaging effects are suggested. These suggestions are intended to stimulate thought and discussion by manufacturers, airworthiness authorities, and others having an interest in finding solutions to the problem; they are intended to serve as a catalyst rather than to lay claim to a definitive solution.

Summary

It was established that the detonation of an IED, loaded in a luggage container positioned on the left side of the forward cargo hold, directly caused the loss of the aircraft. The direct explosive forces produced a large hole in the fuselage structure and disrupted the main cabin floor. Major cracks continued to propagate from the large hole under the influence of the service pressure differential. The indirect explosive effects produced significant structural damage in areas remote from the site of the explosion. The combined effect of the direct and indirect explosive forces was to destroy the structural integrity of the forward fuselage, allow the nose and flight deck area to detach within a period of 2 to 3 seconds, and subsequently allow most of the remaining aircraft to disintegrate while it was descending nearly vertically from 19,000 to 9,000 feet.

The investigation has enabled a better understanding to be gained of the explosive processes involved in such an event and to suggest ways in which the effects of such an explosion might be mitigated, both by changes to future design and also by retrospective modification of aircraft. It is therefore recommended that Regulatory Authorities and aircraft manufacturers undertake a systematic study with a view to identifying measures that might mitigate the effects of explosive devices and improve the tolerance of the aircraft structure and systems to explosive damage.

CONCLUSIONS

CHAPTER 5

CONCLUSIONS

Findings

(i)   The crew were properly licenced and medically fit to conduct the flight.

(ii)   The aircraft had a valid Certificate of Airworthiness and had been maintained in compliance with the regulations.

(iii)   There was no evidence of any defect or malfunction in the aircraft that could have caused or contributed to the accident.

(iv)   The structure was in good condition and the minimal areas of corrosion did not contribute to the in-flight disintegration.

(v)   One minor fatigue crack approximately 3 inches long was found in the fuselage skin but this had not been exploited during the disintegration.

(vi)   An improvised explosive device detonated in luggage container serial number AVE 4041 PA which had been loaded at position 14L in the forward hold. This placed the device approximately 25 inches inboard from the skin on the lower left side of the fuselage at station 700.

(vii)   The analysis of the flight recorders, using currently accepted techniques, did not reveal positive evidence of an explosive event.

(viii)   The direct explosive forces produced a large hole in the fuselage structure and disrupted the main cabin floor. Major cracks continued to propagate from the large hole under the influence of the service pressure differential.

(ix)   The indirect explosive effects produced significant structural damage in areas remote from the site of the explosion.

(x)   The combined effect of the direct and indirect explosive forces was to destroy the structural integrity of the forward fuselage.

(xi)   Containers and items of cargo ejected from the fuselage aperture in the forward hold, together with pieces of detached structure, collided with the empennage severing most of the left tailplane, disrupting the outer half of the right tailplane, and damaging the fin leading edge structure.

(xii)   The forward fuselage and flight deck area separated from the remaining structure within a period of 2 to 3 seconds.

(xiii)   The No 3 engine detached when it was hit by the separating forward fuselage.

(xiv)   Most of the remaining aircraft disintegrated while it was descending nearly vertically from 19,000 to 9,000 feet.

(xv)   The wing impacted in the town of Lockerbie producing a large craterand creating a fireball.

Cause

The in-flight disintegration of the aircraft was caused by the detonation of an improvised explosive device located in a baggage container positioned on the left side of the forward cargo hold at aircraft station 700.

SAFETY RECOMMENDATIONS

CHAPTER 6

SAFETY RECOMMENDATIONS

The following Safety Recommendations were made during the course of the investigation :

1. That manufacturers of existing recorders which use buffering techniques give consideration to making the buffers non-volatile, and the data recoverable after power loss.

2. That Airworthiness Authorities re-consider the concept of allowing buffered data to be stored in a volatile memory.

3. That Airworthiness Authorities consider requiring the CVR system to contain a short duration, i.e. no greater than 1 minute, back-up power supply to enable the CVR to respond to events that result in the almost immediate loss of the aircraft's electrical power supply.

4. That the Department of Transport fund a study to devise methods of recording violent positive and negative pressure pulses, preferably utilising the aircraft's flight recorder systems.

5. That Airworthiness Authorities and aircraft manufacturers

undertake a systematic study with a view to identifying measures that might mitigate the effects of explosive devices and improve the tolerance of aircraft structure and systems to explosive damage.

APPENDICES

APPENDIX A

PERSONNEL CONDUCTING THE INVESTIGATION

The following Inspectors of the Air Accidents Investigation Branch conducted the investigation:

Mr M M Charles	Investigator-in-Charge
Mr D F King	Principal Inspector (Engineering)
Mr P F Sheppard	Assistant Principal Inspector (Engineering)
Mr A N Cable	Senior Inspector (Engineering)
Mr R G Carter	Senior Inspector (Engineering)
Mr P T Claiden	Senior Inspector (Engineering)
Mr P R Coombs	Senior Inspector (Engineering)
Mr S R Culling	Senior Inspector (Engineering)
Miss A Evans	Senior Inspector (Engineering)
Mr B M E Forward	Senior Inspector (Operations)
Mr P N Giles	Senior Inspector (Operations)
Mr S W Moss	Senior Inspector (Engineering)
Mr R Parkinson	Senior Inspector (Engineering)
Mr J D Payling	Senior Inspector (Operations)
Mr C G Pollard	Senior Inspector (Engineering)
Mr C A Protheroe	Senior Inspector (Engineering)
Mr A H Robinson	Senior Inspector (Engineering)
Mr A P Simmons	Senior Inspector (Engineering)
Mr R G Vance	Senior Inspector (Engineering)
Mr R StJ Whidborne	Senior Inspector (Operations)

The Air Accidents Investigation Branch would like to thank the following organisations from the United Kingdom, United States of America, France, and Canada who participated in the investigation:

Air Line Pilot's Association International

Boeing Commercial Airplane Company British Airways
British Army
British Geological Survey Bureau Enquete Accidents
Canadian Aviation Safety Bureau Civil Aviation Authority
Cranfield Institute of Technology Federal Aviation
Administration Federal Bureau of Investigation
Independent Union of Flight Attendants
National Transportation Safety Board Pan American World
Airways Police Service
Royal Aerospace Establishment Royal Air Force
Royal Armaments Research and Development Establishment
Royal Navy
Royal Ordnance
Royal Signals and Radar Establishment
United Technologies International Operations (Pratt and
Whitney)

The Air Accidents Investigation Branch would also like to
acknowledge the excellent work of the Dumfries & Galloway
Regional Council and to thank all the many voluntary organisations
who gave such unstinting support to the investigation.

APPENDIX B

PHOTOGRAPHS AND DIAGRAMS

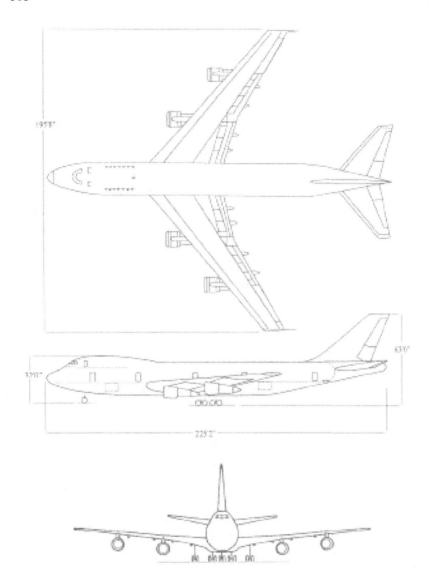

Boeing 747 - 121 Leading Dimensions

Figure B-1

106

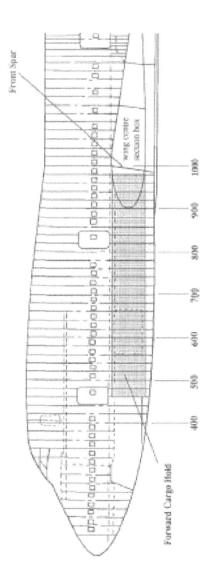

Forward Fuselage Station Diagram

Figure B-2

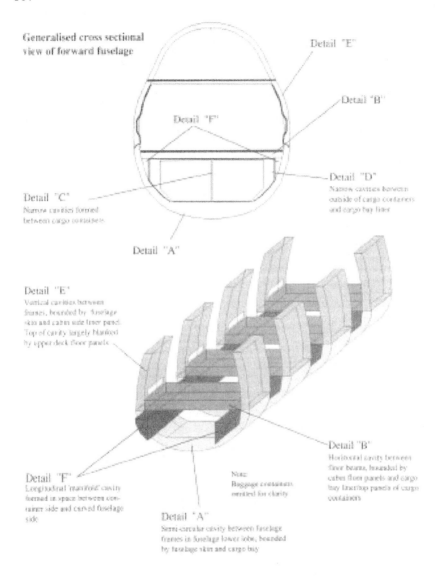

Generalised cross sectional
view of forward fuselage

Detail "E"

Detail "B"

Detail "F"

Detail "D"
Narrow cavities between
outside of cargo containers
and cargo bay liner

Detail "C"
Narrow cavities formed
between cargo containers

Detail "A"

Detail "E"
Vertical cavities between
frames, bounded by fuselage
skin and cabin side liner panel.
Top of cavity largely blanked
by upper deck floor panels

Detail "B"
Horizontal cavity between
floor beams, bounded by
cabin floor panels and cargo
bay liner/top panels of cargo
containers

Detail "F"
Longitudinal 'manifold' cavity
formed in space between container side and curved fuselage
side

Note:
Baggage containers
omitted for clarity

Detail "A"
Semi-circular cavity between fuselage
frames in fuselage lower lobe, bounded
by fuselage skin and cargo bay

Network of Interlinked Cavities
formed within forward fuselage structure and baggage hold
(schematic representation)

Figure B-3

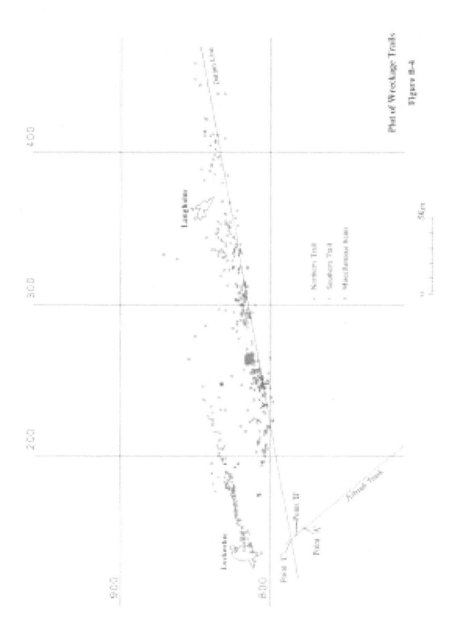

Figure B-4

109

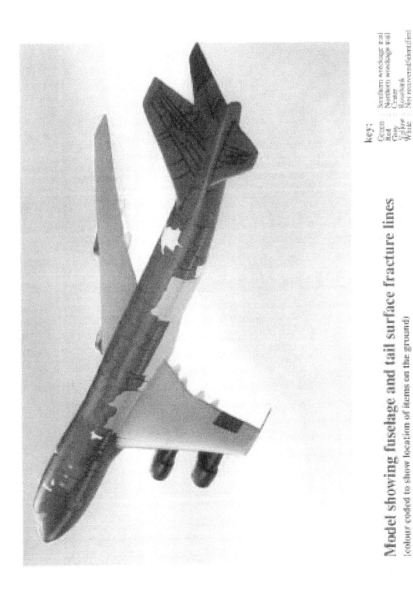

key:
Green : Southern wreckage trail
Red : Northern wreckage trail
Grey : Crater
Yellow : Wreckage
White : Not recovered/identified

Model showing fuselage and tail surface fracture lines
(colour coded to show location of items on the ground)

Figure B-5

110

Model showing fuselage and tail surface fracture lines
(colour coded to show location of items on the ground)

key:

Green : Southern wreckage trail
Red : Northern wreckage trail
Grey : Cream
Yellow : Riverbank
White : Not reconstructed/identified

Figure B-6

111

Model showing fuselage and tail surface fracture lines

(colour coded to show location of items on the ground)

Figure B-7

112

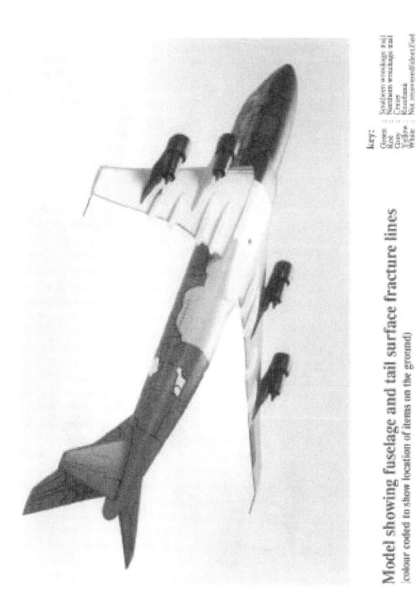

Model showing fuselage and tail surface fracture lines
(colour coded to show location of items on the ground)

key:

Green	Southern wreckage trail
Red	Northern wreckage trail
Grey	Crater
Yellow	Readhouts
White	Not reconciled/collected

Figure B-8

Photograph of nose and flight deck

Figure B-9

114

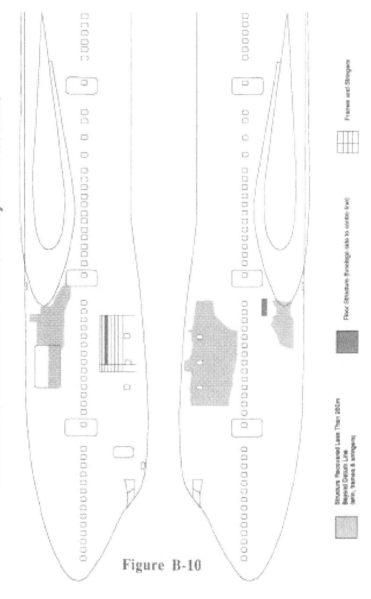

Distribution of Major Wreckage Items Located in Southern Trail.

Structure Recovered Less than 250m Beyond Datum Line

Figure B-10

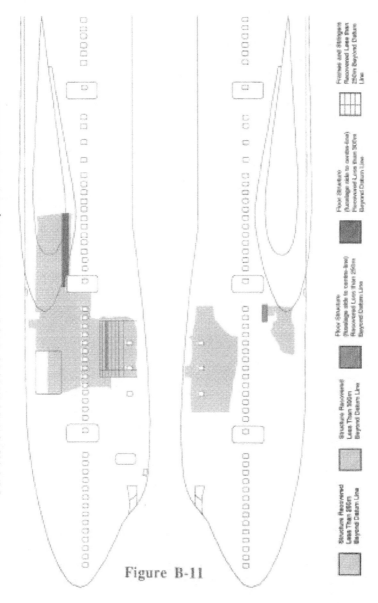

Distribution of Major Wreckage Items Located in Southern Trail.
Structure Recovered Less than 300m Beyond Datum Line

Figure B-11

116

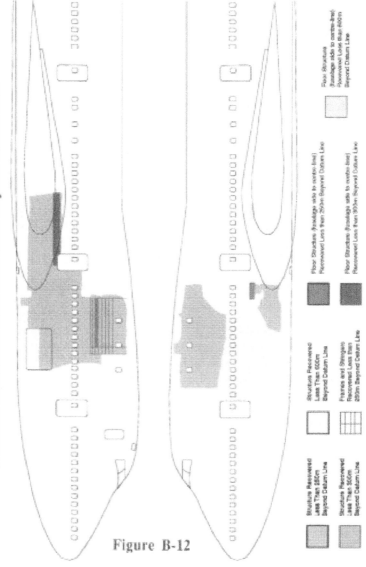

Figure B-12

117

Distribution of Major Wreckage Items Located in Southern Trail.

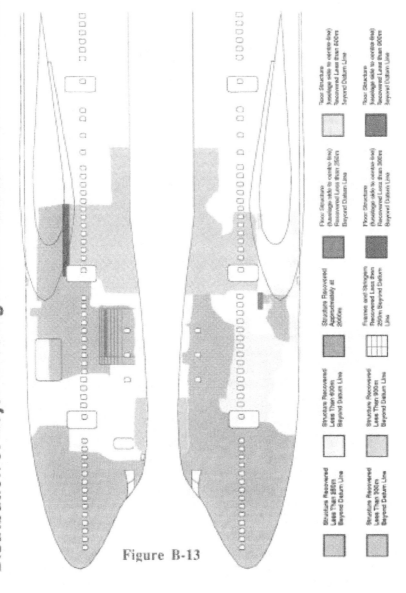

Figure B-13

Two-dimensional layout at CAD Longtown

Figure B-14

Detail of shatter zone of fuselage

Figure B-15

Fuselage three-dimensional reconstruction

Figure B-16

121

Fuselage three-dimensional reconstruction

Figure B-17

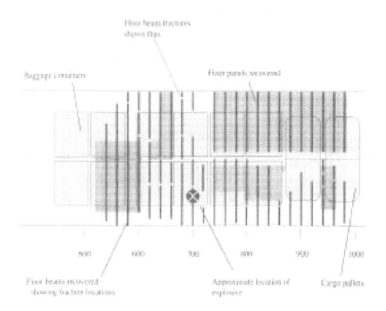

Floor beam fractures
shown thus

Floor panels recovered

Baggage containers

Floor beams recovered
showing fracture locations

500   600   300   800   900   1000

Approximate location of
explosive

Cargo pallets

Plot of floor damage in area of explosion
(structure & floor panel details based on those items recovered, identified, and
incorporated into the three-dimensional reconstruction)

Figure B-18

123

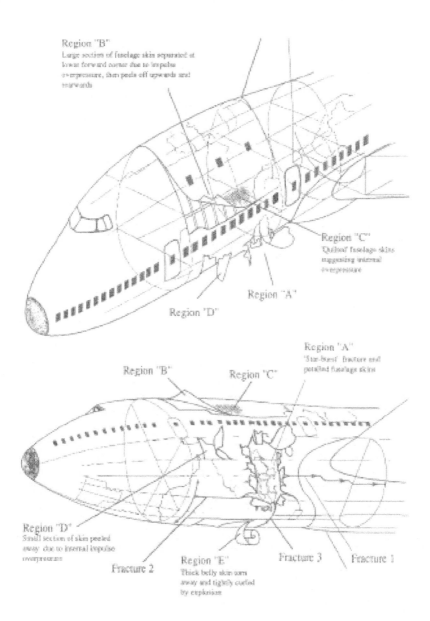

Region "B"
Large section of fuselage skin separated at lower forward corner due to impulse overpressure, then peels off upwards and rearwards

Region "C"
Quilted fuselage skins suggesting internal overpressure

Region "A"

Region "D"

Region "A"
'Star-burst' fracture and petalled fuselage skins

Region "B"

Region "C"

Region "D"
Small section of skin peeled away due to internal impulse overpressure

Region "E"
Thick belly skin torn away and tightly curled by explosion

Fracture 2

Fracture 3

Fracture 1

Explosive Damage - left side
(schematic representation)

Figure B-19

124

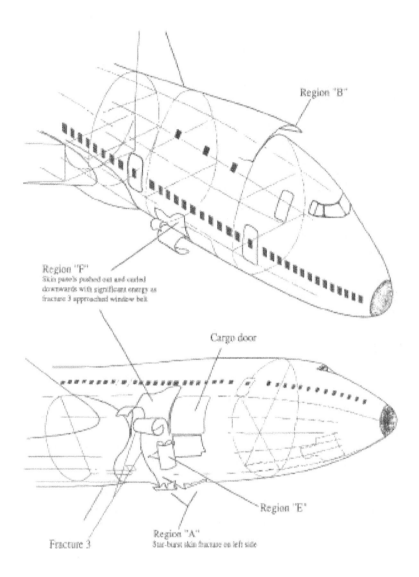

Region "B"

Region "F"
Skin panels pushed out and curled
downwards with significant energy as
fracture 3 approached window belt

Cargo door

Region "E"

Region "A"
Star-burst skin fracture on left side

Fracture 3

Explosive Damage - right side
(schematic representation)

Figure B-20

125

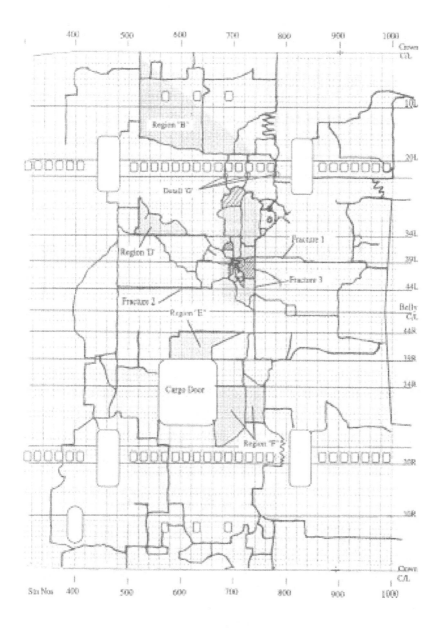

Skin Fracture Plot

Figure B-21

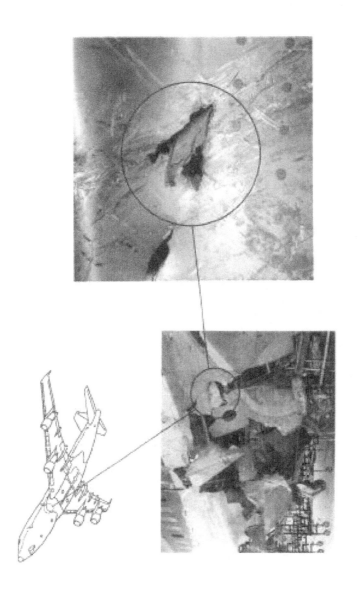

Spar cap embedded in fuselage

Figure B-22

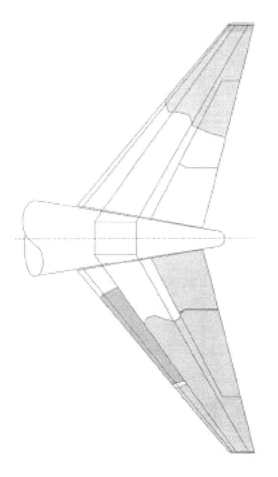

Initial Damage to Tailplanes
(shaded areas denote wreckage recovered from southern wreckage trail)

Figure B-23

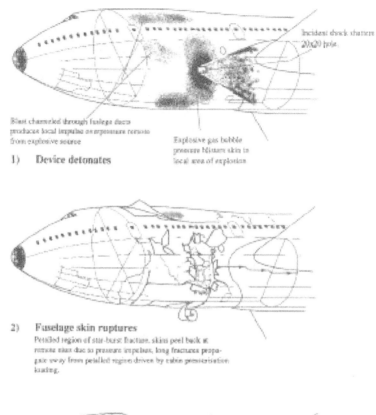

Incident shock shatters
20x20 hole.

Blast channeled through fuselage ducts
produces local impulse on exposure remote
from explosive source

Explosive gas bubble
pressure blitzes skin in
local area of explosion

1) Device detonates

2) Fuselage skin ruptures

Petalled region of star-burst fracture, skins peel back at
remote sites due to pressure impulses, long fractures propagate away from petalled region driven by cabin pressurisation
loading.

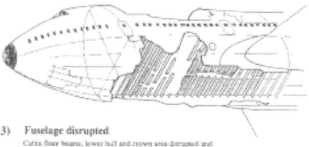

3) Fuselage disrupted

Cabin floor beams, lower hull and crown area disrupted and
structure separated; nose section retained by window belts only.

Fuselage Initial Damage Sequence
(schematic representation)

Figure B-24

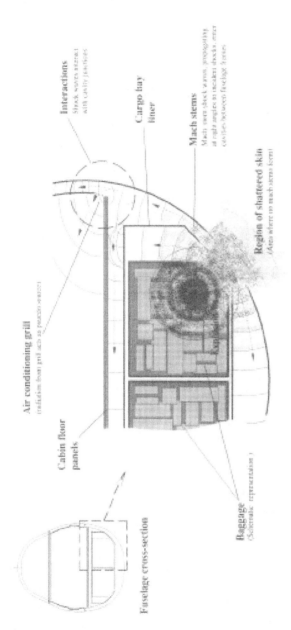

Air conditioning grill
(radiates heat grill acts as reaction source)

Interactions
Shock waves interact with cavity junctions

Cabin floor panels

Cargo bay liner

Mach stems
Mach stem shock waves, propagating at right angles to incident shocks, enter cavities between fuselage frames

Baggage
(Schematic representation)

Region of shattered skin
(Area where up mach stems form)

Fuselage cross-section

Incident Shock & Regions of Mach Stem Propagation
(schematic representation)

Figure B-25

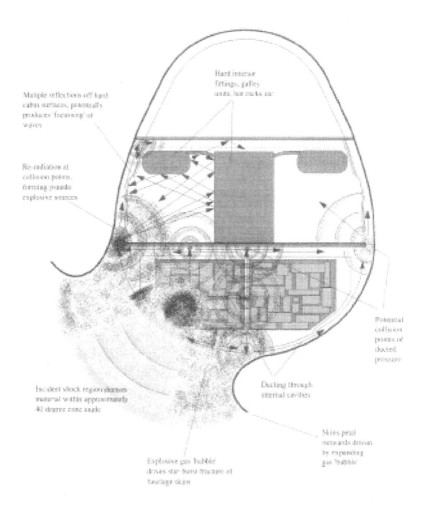

Potential Shock and Explosive Gas Propagation Paths
(schematic representation)

Figure B-26

APPENDIX C

ANALYSIS OF RECORDED DATA

1. Introduction

This appendix describes and analyses the different types of recorded data which were examined during the investigation of the accident to Boeing 747 registration N739PA at Lockerbie on 21 December 1988. The recorded data consists of that from the Cockpit Voice Recorder (CVR), the Digital Flight Data Recorder (DFDR), Air Traffic Control (ATC) radio telephony (RTF), ATC radar, and British Geological Survey seismic records. The time correlation of the records is also discussed.

2. Digital flight data recorder

The flight data recorder installation conformed to ARINC 573B standard with a Lockheed Model 209 DFDR receiving data from a Teledyne Controls Flight Data Acquisition Unit (FDAU). The system recorded 22 analogue parameters and 27 discrete (event) parameters. The flight recorder control panel was located in the flight deck overhead panel. The FDAU was in the main equipment centre at the front end of the forward hold and the flight recorder was mounted in the aft equipment centre.

2.1. DFDR strip and examination

Internal inspection of the DFDR showed that there was considerable disruption to the control electronics circuits. The crash protection was removed and the plastic recording tape was found detached from its various guide rollers and tangled in the tape spools. There was no tension in the negator springs. This indicated that the tape had probably moved since electrical power was removed from the recorder. The position of the tape in relation to the record/replay heads was marked with a piece of splicing tape in order to quantify the movement. To ensure that no additional damage was caused to the tape it was necessary to cut the negator springs to separate the upper and lower tape reels.

The crinkling and stretching of the tape and the damage to the control electronics meant that the tape had to be replayed outside the recorder. AAIB experience has shown that the most efficient method of replaying stretched Lockheed recorder tapes is to re-spool the tape into a known serviceable recorder, in this case a Plessey 1584 g.

2.2 DFDR replay

The 25 hour duration of the DFDR was satisfactorily replayed. Data relating to the accident flight was recorded on track 2. The only significant defect in the recording system was that normal acceleration was inoperative. There was one area on the tape, 2 minutes from the end, where data synchronisation was lost for 1 second.

Decoding and reduction of the data from the accident flight showed that no abnormal behaviour of the data sensors had been recorded. The recorded data simply stopped. Figure C-1 is a graphical representation of the main flight parameters.

2.3 DFDR analysis

In order to ensure that all recorded data from the accident flight had been decoded and to examine the quality of the data at the end of the recording, a section of tape, including both the most recently recorded data and the oldest data (data from 25 hours past), was replayed through an ultra-violet (UV) strip recorder. The data was also digitised and the resulting samples used to reconstruct the tape signal on a VDU.

Both methods of signal representation were used to determine the manner by which the recorder stopped. There was no gap between the most recently recorded data and the 25 hour old data. This showed that the recorder stopped while there was an incoming data stream from the FDAU. The recorder, therefore, stopped because its electrical supply was disconnected. The tape signal was examined for any transients or noise signals that would have indicated the presence of electrical disturbances prior to the recorder stopping. None was found and this indicated that there had been a quick clean break of the electrical supply.

The last seconds of data were decoded independently using both the UV record and the digitised signal. Only 17 bits of data were not recoverable (less that 23 milliseconds) and it was not possible to establish with any certainty if this data was from the accident flight or if it was old data from a previous recording.

A working group of the European Organisation for Civil Aviation Electronics (EUROCAE) was, during the period of the investigation, formulating new standards (Minimum Operational Performance Requirement for Flight Data Recorder Systems, Ref:- ED55) for future generation flight recorders which would have permitted delays between parameter input and recording (buffering) of up to $^1/2$ second. These standards are intended to form the basis of new CAA specifications for flight recorders and may be adopted worldwide.

The analysis of the final data recorded on the DFDR was possible because the system did not buffer the incoming data.

Some existing recorders use a process whereby data is stored temporarily in a memory device (buffer) before recording. The data within this buffer is lost when power is removed from the recorder and in currently designed recorders this may mean that up to 1.2 seconds of final data contained within the buffer is lost. Due to the necessary processing of the signals prior to input to the recorder, additional delays of up to 300 milliseconds may be introduced. If the accident had occurred when tha aircraft was over the sea, it is very probable that the relatively few small items of structure, luggage and clothing showing positive evidence of the detonation of an explosive device would not have been recovered. However, as flight recorders are fitted with underwater location beacons, there is a high probability that they would have been located and recovered. In such an event the final milliseconds of data contained on the DFDR could be vital to the successful determination of the cause of an accident whether due to an explosive device or other catastrophic failure. Whilst it may not be possible to reduce some of the delays external to the recorder, it is possible to reduce any data loss due to buffering of data within the data acquisition unit.

It is, therefore, recommended that manufacturers of existing recorders which use buffering techniques give consideration to making the buffers non-volatile, and hence recoverable after power loss. Although the recommendation on this aspect, made to the EUROCAE working group during the investigation, was incorporated into ED55, it is also recommended that Airworthiness Authorities reconsider the concept of allowing buffered data to be stored in a volatile memory.

3. Cockpit voice recorder (CVR)

The aircraft was equipped with a 30 minute duration 4 track Fairchild Model A100 CVR, and a Fairchild model A152 cockpit area microphone (CAM). The CVR control panel containing the CAM was located in the overhead panel on the flight deck and the recorder itself was mounted in the aft equipment centre.

The channel allocation was as follows:-

Channel 1   Flight Engineer's RTF.
Channel 2   Co-Pilot's RTF.
Channel 3   Pilot's RTF.
Channel 4   Cockpit Area Microphone

3.1 CVR strip and examination

To gain access to the recording tape it was necessary to cut away the the outer case and saw through part of the crash protected enclosure. No damage to the tape transport or the recording tape was found. The endless loop of tape was cut and the tape transferred to the replay equipment. The electronic modules in the CVR were crushed and there was evidence of long term overheating of the dropper resistors on the power supply module. The CAM had been crushed breaking internal wiring and damaging components on the printed circuit board.

3.2 CVR replay

The erase facility within the CVR was not functioning satisfactorily and low level communications from earlier recordings was audible on the RTF channels. The CAM channel was particularly noisy, this was probably due to the combination of the inherently noisy cockpit of the B747-100 in the climb and distortion from the incomplete erasure of the previous recordings. On two occasions the crew had difficulty understanding ATC, possibly indicating high cockpit noise levels. There was a low frequency sound present at irregular intervals on the CAM track but the source of this sound could not be identified as of either acoustic or electrical in origin.

The CVR tape was listened to for its full duration and there was no indication of anything abnormal with the aircraft, or unusual in crew behaviour. The tape record ended with a sudden loud sound on the CAM channel followed almost immediately by the cessation of recording. The sound occurred whilst the crew were copying their transatlantic clearance from Shanwick ATC.

3.3   Analysis of the CVR record

3.3.1 The stopping of the recorder

To determine the mechanism that stopped the recorder a bench test rig was constructed utilizing an A100 CVR and an A152 CAM. Figures C-2 to C-5 show the effect of shorting, earthing or disconnecting the CAM signal wires. Figure C8 shows the CAM channel signal response to the event which occurred on Flight PA103. From this it can be seen that there are no characteristic transients similar to those caused by shorting or earthing the CAM signal wires. Neither does the signal stop cleanly and quickly as shown in Figure C-5, indicating that the CAM signal wires were not interrupted. The UV trace shows the recorded signal decaying in a manner similar to that shown in Figure C-6, which demonstrates the effect of disconnecting electrical power from the recorder. The tests were repeated on other CVRs with similar results and it is therefore concluded that Flight PA103's CVR stopped because its electrical power was removed.

Figures C-9A to C-9D show the recorded signals for the Air India B747 (AI 182) accident in the North Atlantic on 23 June 1985. These show that there is a large transient on the CAM track indicating earthing or shorting of the CAM signal wires and that recorder power-down is more prolonged, indicating attempts to restore the electrical power supply either by bus switching or healing of the fault. The Flight PA103 CVR shows no attempts at power restoration with the break being clean and final.

In order to respond to events that result in the almost immediate loss of the aircraft's electrical power supply it was therefore recommended during the investigation that the regulatory authorities consider requiring CVR systems to contain a short duration (i.e. no greater than 1 minute) back-up power supply.

3.3.2 Information concerning the event

Figure C-8 is an expanded UV trace of the final milliseconds of the CVR record. Three tracks have been used, the flight engineer's RTF channel which contained similar information to the P2's channel has been replaced with a timing signal. Individual sections of interest are identified by number. On the bottom trace, the P1 RTF track, section 1 is part of the Shanwick transatlantic clearance. During this section the loud sound on the CAM channel is evident.

Examination of the DFDR event recordings shows that the Shanwick oceanic clearance was being received on VHF2, the aerial for which is on the underside of the fuselage close to the seat of the explosion. Section 2 identifies a transient, on the P1 channel, typical of an end of ATC transmission transient for this CVR. The start and finish of most of the recorded ATC transmissions were analysed and they produce a similar signature to the three shown in Figure C-10. The signature on the P1 channel more closely resembles the end of transmission signature and it is open to conjecture that this transient was caused by the explosion damaging the aerial feeder and/or its supporting structure.

Section 3 shows what is considered to be a high speed power supply transient which is evident on all the RTF channels and is probably on the CAM channel, but cannot be identified because of the automatic gain control (AGC), limiting the audio event. This transient is considered to coincide with the loss of electrical power to the CVR. Section 5 identifies the period to the end of recording and this agrees well with tests carried out by AAIB and independently by Fairchild as part of the AI 182 investigation. The typical time from removal of the electrical supply until end of recording is 110 milliseconds.

During the period identified as section 4 it is considered that the disturbances on the RTF channels are electrical transients probably channelled through the communications equipment. Section 6 identifies the 170 millisecond period from the point when the sound was first heard on the CAM until the recording stopped.

The CAM unit is of the old type which has a frequency response of 350 to 3500 Hz. The useable duration of the signal is probably confined to the first 60 milliseconds of the final 170 milliseconds and even during this period the AGC is limiting the signal. In the remaining time the sound is being distorted because power to the recorder has been disconnected. The ambient cockpit noise may have been high enough to have caused the AGC to have been active prior to the event and in this event the full volume of the sound would not be audible. Distortion from the incomplete erasure of the last recording may form part of the recorded signal.

It is not clear if the recorded sound is the result of the explosion or is from the break-up of the aircraft structure. The short period between the beginning of the event and the loss of electrical power suggests that the latter is more likely to be the case.

Additionally some of the frequencies present on the recording were not present in the original sound, but are the result of the rise in total harmonic distortion caused by the increased amplitude of the incoming signal. Outputs from a frequency analysis of the recorded signal for the same frequency of input to the CVR, but at two input amplitudes, are shown in Figures C-11 and C-12. These illustrate the effects on harmonic distortion as the signal level is increased. Finally the recorded signal does not lend itself to analysis by a digital spectrum analyser as it is, in a large measure, aperiodic and most digital signal analysis algorithms are unable to deal with a short duration signal of this type, however, it is hoped that techniques being developed in Canada will enable more information to be deduced from the end of the recording.

In the aftermath of the Air India Boeing 747 accident (AI 182) in the North Atlantic on 23 June 1985 the Royal Armaments Research and Development Establishment (RARDE) were asked informally by AAIB to examine means of differentiating, by recording violent cabin pressure pulses, between the detonation of an explosive device within the cabin (positive pulse) and a catastrophic structural failure (negative pulse). Following the Lockerbie disaster it was considered that this work should be raised to a formal research project. Therefore, in February 1989, it was recommended that the Department of Transport fund a study to devise methods of recording violent positive and negative pressure pulses, preferably utilising the aircraft's flight recorder systems.

Preliminary results from these trials indicates that if a suitable sensor can be developed its output will need to be recorded in real time and therefore it may require wiring into the CVR installation. This will further strengthen the requirement for battery back up of the CVR electrical power supply.

4. Flight recorder electrical system

4.1 CVR/DFDR electrical wiring.

The flight recorders were located in the left rear fuselage just forward of the rear pressure bulkhead. Audio information to the CVR ran along the left hand side of the aircraft, at stringer 11. Electrical power to the CVR followed a similar route on the right hand side of the aircraft crossing to the left side above the rear passenger toilets. DFDR electrical power and signal information followed the same route as the CVR audio information.

4.2 Flight recorder power supply

The DFDR, CVR and the transponders were all powered from the essential alternating current (AC) bus. This bus was capable of being powered by any generator, however, in normal operation the selector switch on the flight engineers panel is selected to "normal" connecting the essential bus to number 4 generator. When the cockpit of Flight PA 103 was examined the selector switch was found in the normal position.

4.3 Aircraft alternating current power supplies

AC electrical power to the aircraft was provided by 4 engine driven generators, see Figure C-13. Each generator was driven at constant speed through a constant speed drive (CSD) and connected to a separate bus-bar through a generator control breaker (GCB). The 4 generators were connected to a parallel bus-bar (sync bus) by individual bus tie breakers (BTBs). Control and monitoring of the AC electrical system was achieved through the flight engineer's instrument panel. In normal operation the generators operated in parallel, i.e with the BTBs closed.

4.4 Fault conditions

Analysis of the CVR CAM channel signal indicated that approximately 60 milliseconds after the sound on the CAM channel an electrical transient was recorded on all 4 channels and that approximately 110 milliseconds later the CVR had ceased recording. Within the accuracy of the available timing information it is believed that the incoming VHF was lost at the same time, indicating an AC power supply fault.

The AC electrical system was protected from faults in individual systems or equipment by fuses or circuit breakers. Faults in the generators or in the distribution bus-bars and feeders were dealt with automatically by opening of the GCBs and opening or closing of the BTBs. In the event of fault conditions causing the disconnection of all 4 generators electrical power for essential services, including VHF radio, was provided by a battery located in the cockpit.

The short time interval of 55 milliseconds after which the AC supply to the flight recorders was lost limits the basis on which a fault path analysis of the AC electrical system can be undertaken. On the available information only a differential (feeder) fault could have isolated the bus-bar this quickly, with the generator field control relay taking 20 milliseconds to trip. However, in normal operation, the generators would have been operating in parallel and the essential AC bus-bar would have been supplied via the number 4 BTB from the sync bus. If the fault conditions had continued, a further 40 to 100 milliseconds would have elapsed before the BTB opened. If the BTB was open prior to the fault it would have attempted to close and restore the supply to the essential bus. Any automatic switching causes electrical transients to appear on the CVR and data losses on the FDR. Both the CVR and the FDR indicate that a clean break of the AC supply occurred with no electrical transients associated with BTBs open or closing in an attempt to restore power. In the absence of any additional information only two possibilities are apparent:

a. That all 4 generators were simultaneously affected causing a total loss of AC electrical power. The feeders for the left and right side generators run on opposite sides of the aircraft under the passenger cabin floor. The only situation envisaged that could cause simultaneous loss of all 4 generators is the disruption of the passenger cabin floor across its entire width.

b. That disruption of the main equipment centre, housing the control units for the AC electrical system, caused the loss of all AC power. However, again it would have to affect both the left and right sides of the aircraft as the control equipment is located at left and right extremes of the main equipment centre.

The nature of the event may also produce effects that are not understood. It is also to be noted that a sudden loss of electrical power to the flight recorders has been reported in other B747 accidents, e.g. Air India, AI 182.

5. Seismic Data

The British Geological Survey has a number of seismic monitoring stations in Southern Scotland. Stations close to Lockerbie recorded a seismic event caused by the wing section crashing on Lockerbie. The seismic monitors are time correlated with the British Telecom Rugby standard. Using this and calculating the time for the various waves to reach the recording stations it was possible for the British Geological Survey to conclude that the event occurred at 19.03:36.5 hrs ± 1 second.

Attempts were made to correlate various smaller seismic events with other wreckage impacts. However, this was not conclusive because the nearest recording station was above ground and due to the high winds at the time of the accident had considerable noise on the trace. In addition, little of the other wreckage had the mass or impact velocity to stimulate the sensors.

6. Time correlation

6.1 Introduction

The sources of each time encoded recording were asked to provide details of their time standard and any known errors in the timings on their recordings. Although the resolution of the recorded time sources is high it was not possible to attach an accuracy of better than ±1 second due to possible errors in synchronising the recorded time with the associated standard. The following time sources were available and used in determining the significant events in the investigation:-

i. ATC

ATC communications were recorded along with a time signal. The time source for the ATC tape was the British Telecom "Tim" signal. Any error in setting the time when individual tapes are mounted was logged.

ii. Recorded rada data

A time signal derived from the British Telecom "Rugby" standard was included on radar recordings. The Rugby and Tim times were assumed to be of equal accuracy for timing purposes.

iii The DFDR had UTC recorded.

The source of this time was the flight engineer's clock. This clock was set manually and therefore this time was subject to a significant fixed error as well any inaccuracy in the clock.

iv. The CVR had no time signal.

However, the CVR was correlated with the ATC time through the RTF and with the DFDR, by correlating the press to talk events on the FDR with the press to talk signature on the CVR.

v.Seismic recordings

Seismic recordings included a timing signal derived from the British Telecom Rugby standard.

6.2 Analysis and correlation of times

The Scottish and Shanwick ATC tapes were matched with each other and with the CVR tape. The CVR recording speed was adjusted by peaking its recorded 400 Hz AC power source frequency. This correlation served as a double check on any fixed errors on the ATC recordings and to fix events on the CVR to UTC. The timing of the sound on the CAM channel of the CVR was made simpler because Shanwick was transmitting when it occurred. From this it was possible to determine that the sound on the CVR occurred at 19.02:50 hrs ±1 second.

With the CVR now tied to the Tim standard it was possible to match the RTF keying on the CVR with the RTF keying events on the FDR. These events on the FDR were sampled and recorded once per second, it was therefore possible for a 1 second delay to be present on the FDR. This potential error was reduced by obtaining the best fit between a number of RTF keyings and a time correlation between the FDR and CVR of ±'4 second was achieved. From this it was determined, within this accuracy, that electrical power was removed from the CVR and FDR at the same time.

From the recorded radar data it was possible to determine that the last recorded SSR return was at 19.02:46.9 hrs and that by the next rotation of the radar head a number of primary returns, some left and right of track, were evident. Time intervals between successive rotations of the radar head became more difficult to use as the head painted more primary returns.

The point at which aircraft wreckage impacted Lockerbie was determined using the time recorded by seismic activity detectors. A seismic event measuring 1.6 on the Richter scale was detected and, with appropriate time corrections for times of the waves to reach the sensors, it was established that this occurred at 19.03:36.5 hrs ±1 second. A further check was made by triangulation techniques from the information recorded by the various sensors.

7 . Recorded radar information

7.1 Introduction

Recorded radar information on the aircraft was available from from 4 radar sites. Initial analysis consisted of viewing the recorded information as it was shown to the controller on the radar screen, from this it was clear that the flight had progressed in a normal manner until Secondary Surveillance Radar (SSR) was lost. There was a single primary return received by both Great Dun Fell and Claxby radars approximately 16 seconds before SSR returns were lost. The Lowther Hill and St. Annes radars did not see this return. The Great Dun Fell radar recording was watched for 1 hour both before and after this single return for any signs of other spurious returns, but none was seen. The return was only present for one paint and no explanation can be offered for its presence.

7.2 Limitations of recorded radar data

Before evaluating the recorded radar data it is important to highlight limitations in radar performance that must be taken into account when interpreting primary radar data. The radar system used for both primary and secondary radar utilised a rotating radar transmitter/receiver (Head). This means that a return was only visible whilst the radar head was pointing at the target, commonly called painting or illuminating the target. In the case of this accident the rotational speeds of the radar heads varied from approximately 10 seconds for the Lowther Hill Radar to 8 Seconds for the Great Dun Fell Radar.

Whilst it was possible to obtain accurate positional information within a resolution of 0.09° of bearing and ± 1/16 nautical mile range for an aircraft from SSR, incorporating mode C height encoding, primary radar provided only slant range and bearing and therefore positional information with respect to the ground was not accurate.

The structural break-up of an aircraft releases many items which were excellent radar reflectors eg. aluminium cladding, luggage containers, sections of skin and aircraft structure. These and other debris with reflective properties produce "clutter" on the radar by confusing the radar electronics in a manner similar to chaff ejected by military aircraft to avoid radar detection.

Even when the target is not masked by clutter repetitive detection of individual targets may not be possible because detection is a function of the target effective area which, for wreckage with its irregular shape, is not constant but fluctuates wildly. These factors make it impossible to follow individual returns through successive sweeps of the radar head.

7.3 Analysis of the radar data

The detailed analysis of the radar information concentrated on the break-up of the aircraft. The Royal Signals and Radar Establishment (RSRE) corrected the radar returns for fixed errors and converted the SSR returns to latitude and longitude so that an accurate time and position for the aircraft could be determined. This information was correlated with the CVR and ATC times to establish a time and position for the aircraft at the initial disintegration.

For the purposes of this analysis the data from Great Dun Fell Radar has been presented. Figures C-14 to C-23 show a mosaic picture of the radar data i.e. each figure contains the information on the preceding figure together with more recently recorded information. Figure C-14 shows the radar returns from an aircraft tracking 321°(Grid) with a calculated ground speed of 434 kts. Reading along track (towards the top left of Figure C-14) there are 6 SSR returns with the sixth and final SSR return shown decoded: squawk code 0357 (identifying the aircraft as N739PA); mode C indicating FL310; and the time in seconds (68566.9 seconds from 00:00, i.e. 19.02:46.9 hrs).

At the next radar return there is no SSR data, only 4 primary returns. One return is along track close to the expected position of the aircraft if it had continued at its previous speed and heading. There are 2 returns to the left of track and 1 to the right of track. Remembering the point made earlier about clutter, it is unlikely that each of these returns are real targets. It can, however, be concluded that the aircraft is no longer a single return and, considering the approximately 1 nautical mile spread of returns across track, that items have been ejected at high speed probably to both right and left of the aircraft. Figure C-15 shows the situation after the next head rotation. There is still a return along track but it has either slowed down or the slant range has decreased due to a loss of altitude.

Each rotation of the radar head thereafter shows the number

of returns increasing with those first identified across track in Figure C-14 having slowed down very quickly and followed a track along the prevailing wind line. Figure C-20 shows clearly that there has been a further break-up of the aircraft and subsequent plots show a rapidly increasing number of returns, some following the wind direction and forming a wreckage trail parallel to and north of the original break-up debris. Additionally it is possible that there was some break-up between these points with a short trail being formed between the north and south trails. From the absence of any returns travelling along track it can be concluded that the main wreckage was travelling almost vertically downwards for much of the time.

The geographical position of the final secondary return at 19.02:46.9 hrs was calculated by RSRE to be OS Grid Reference 15257772, annotated Point A in Appendix B, Figure B-4, with an accuracy considered to be better than ±300 metres This return was received 3.1±1 seconds before the loud sound was recorded on the CVR at 19.02:50 hrs. By projecting from this position along the track of 321°(Grid) for 3.1±1 seconds at the groundspeed of 434 kts, the position of the aircraft was calculated to be OS Grid Reference 14827826, annotated Point B in Appendix B, Figure B-4, within an accuracy of ±525 metres. Based on the evidence of recorded data only, Point B therefore represents the geographical position of the aircraft at the moment the loud sound was recorded on the CVR.

8. Conclusions

The almost instant destruction of Flight PA103 resulted in no direct evidence on the cause of the accident being preserved on the DFDR. The CVR CAM track contained a loud sound 170 milliseconds before recording ceased. Sixty milliseconds of this sound were while power was applied to the recorder; after this period the amplitude decreased. It cannot be determine whether the decrease was because of reducing recorder drive or if the sound itself decreased in amplitude. Analysis of both flight recorders shows that they stopped because the electrical supply was removed and that there were valid signals available to both recorders at that time.

The most important contribution to the investigation that the flight recorders could make was to pinpoint the time and position of the event. As the timescale involved was so small in relation to the resolution and accuracy of many of the recorded time sources it was necessary to analyse collectively all the available recordings. From the analysis of the CVR, DFDR, ATC tapes, radar data and the seismic records it was concluded that the loud sound on the CVR occurred at 19.02:50 hrs ±1 second and wreckage from the aircraft crashed on Lockerbie at 19.03:36.5 hrs ±1 second, giving a time interval of 46.5 ±2 seconds between these two events. When the loud sound was recorded on the CVR, the geographical position of the aircraft, based on the evidence of recorded data, was calculated to be within 525 metres of OS Grid Reference 14827826.

Eight seconds after the sound on the CVR the Great Dun Fell radar showed 4 primary radar returns. The returns indicated a spread of wreckage in the order of 1 nautical mile across track. On successive returns of the radar, two parallel wreckage trails are seen to develop with the second trail, to the north, becoming evident 30 to 40 seconds after the first.

150

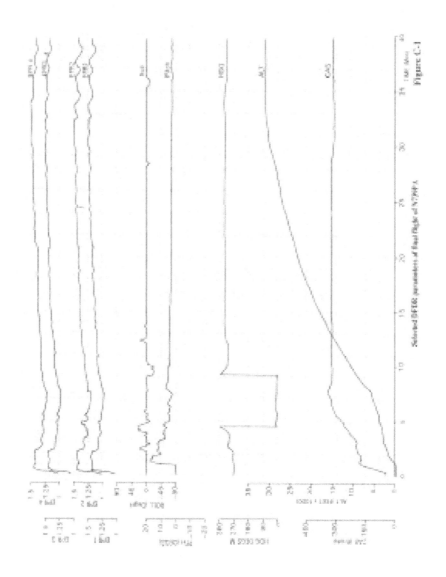

Selected BHTSE parameters of Final flight of N749A

Figure C-1

151

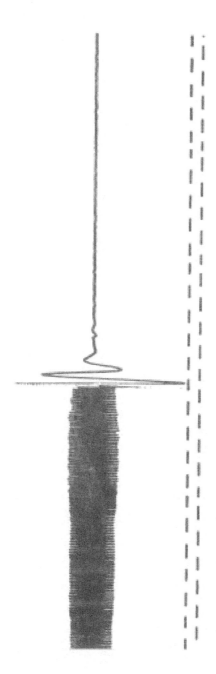

The effect on the recorded signal of shorting the signal wires to the CAM

Figure C-2

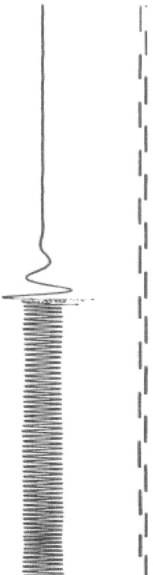

The effect on the recorded signal of earthing the hi wire to the CAM

Figure C-3

153

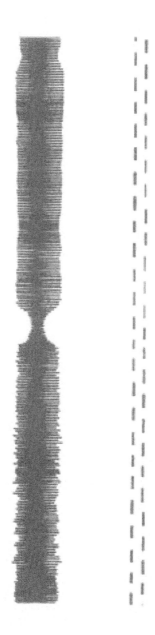

The effect on the recorded signal of earthing the lo wire to the CAM

Figure C-4

154

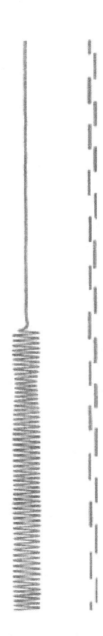

The effect on the recorded signal of disconnecting the CAM signal wires

Figure C-5

The effect on the recorded CAM signal of disconnecting the CVR power supply

Figure C-6

156

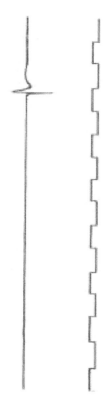

Figure C-7

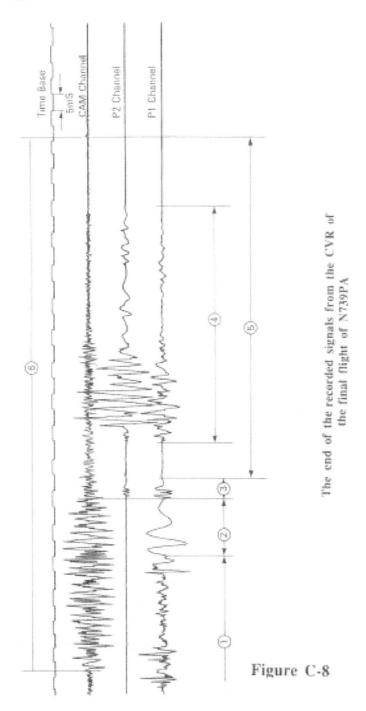

The end of the recorded signals from the CVR of
the final flight of N739PA

Figure C-8

CVR TIME HISTORY

Analogue Output of all 4 Tracks
Each Strip Approx. 410 milliseconds

Area MIC

Captain's RTF

Co-pilot's RTF

Flt Eng.'s RTF

Figure C-9A

Timebase

0   mSec   100

The final CVR signals from Air India Flight 182

159

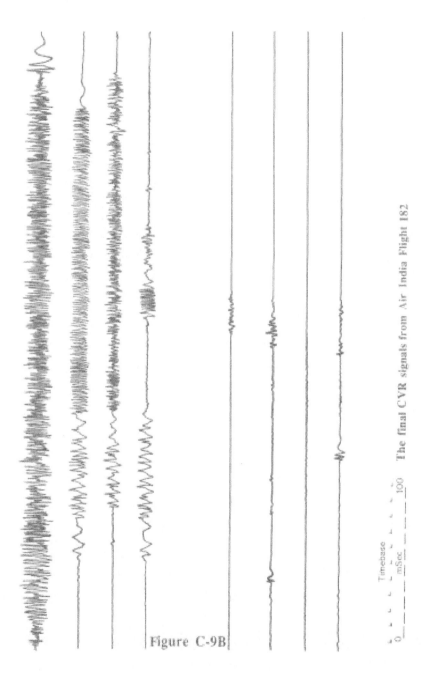

Figure C-9B

Timebase
0   mSec   100   The final CVR signals from Air India Flight 182

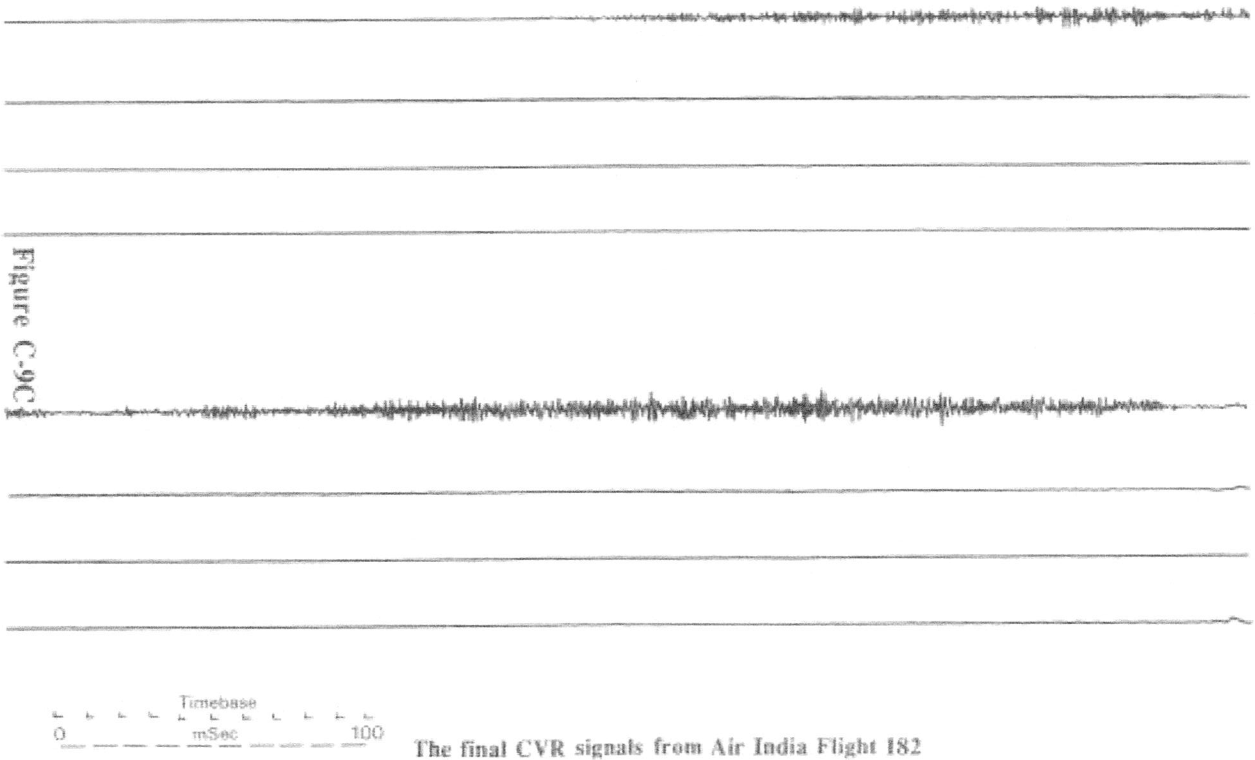

Figure C-9C

Timebase
0 _____ mSec _____ 100

The final CVR signals from Air India Flight 182

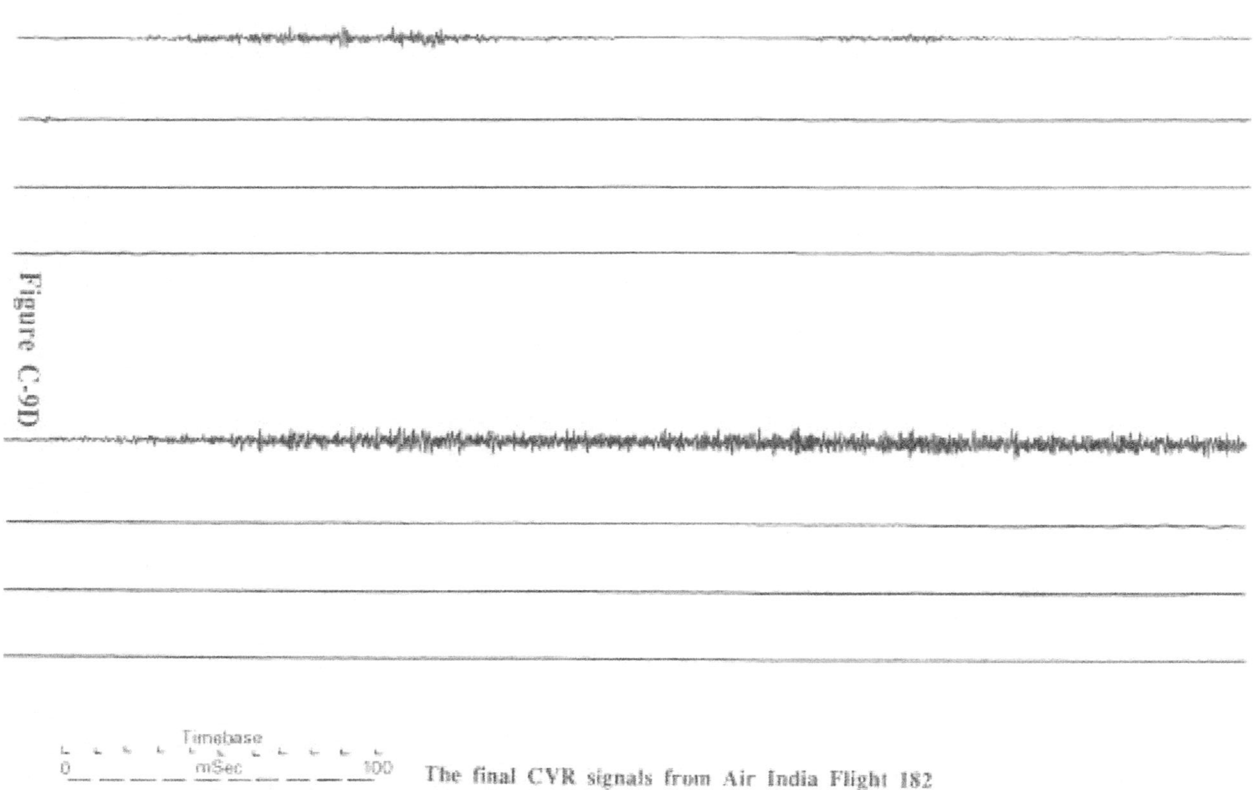

161

Figure C-9D

Timebase
mSec   100

The final CVR signals from Air India Flight 182

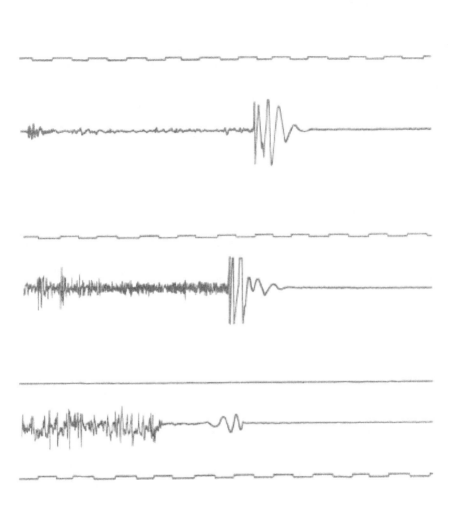

Three typical end of RTF transmission transients
from N739PA, recorded on the CVR

Figure C-10

163

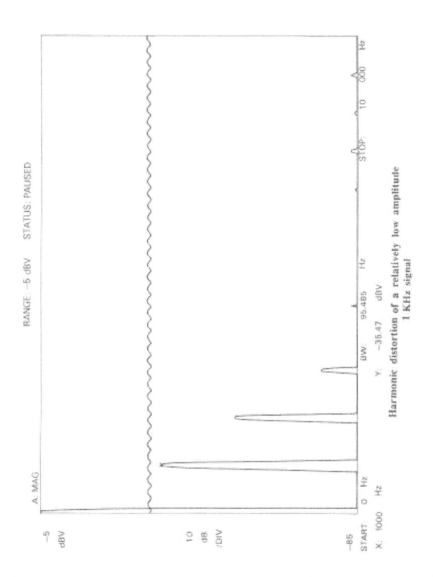

Figure C-11

164

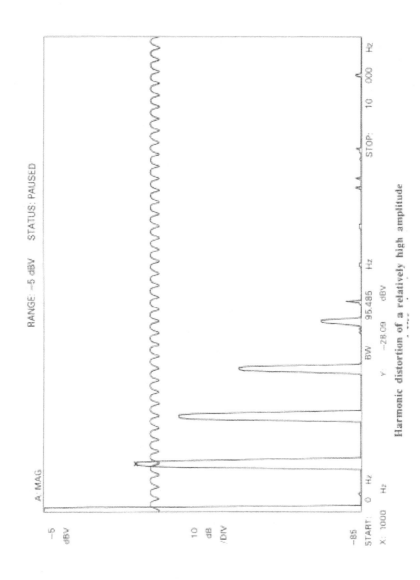

Figure C-12

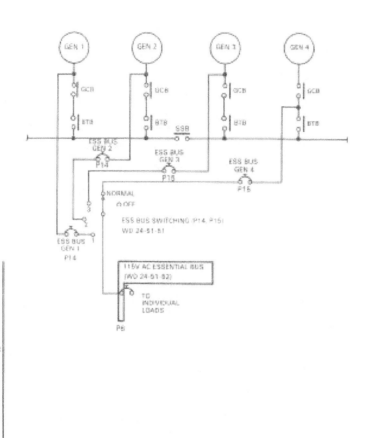

Boeing 747 main 115 volt AC power load distribution

Figure C-13

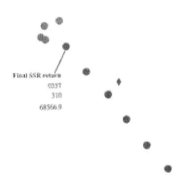

Final SSR return
0357
310
68566.9

Time Secs = 68578

1st Primary Added

Radar returns from the final flight of N739PA

Figures C-14

167

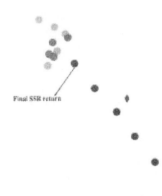

Final SSR return

Time Secs = 68586

2nd Primary Added

Radar returns from the final flight of N739PA

Figures C-15

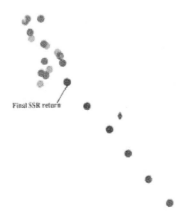

Final SSR return

Time Secs = 68594

3rd Primary Added

Radar returns from the final flight of N739PA

Figures C-16

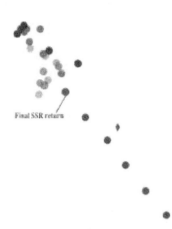

Final SSR return

Time Secs = 68599

4th Primary Added

Radar returns from the final flight of N739PA

Figures C-17

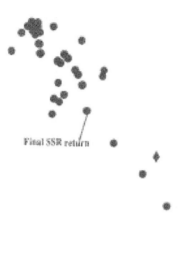

Final SSR return

Time Secs = 68610

5th Primary Added

Radar returns from the final flight of N739PA

Figures C-18

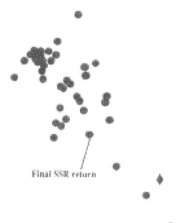

Final SSR return

Time Secs = 68618

6th Primary Added

Radar returns from the final flight of N739PA

Figures C-19

Final SSR return

Time Secs = 68627

7th Primary Added

Radar returns from the final flight of N739PA

Figures C-20

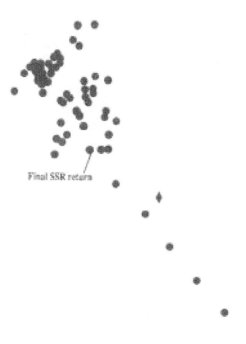

Final SSR return

Time Secs = 68635

8th Primary Added

Radar returns from the final flight of N739PA

Figures C-21

174

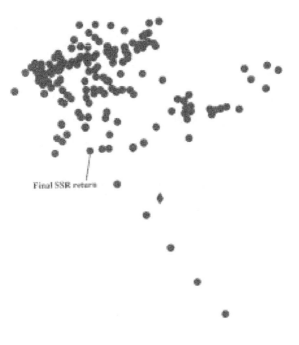

Final SSR return

Time Secs = 68753

Radar returns from the final flight of N739PA

Figures C-22

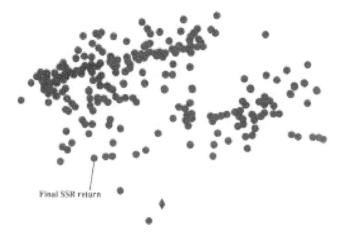

Final SSR return

Time Secs = 68816

Radar returns from the final flight of N739PA

Figures C-23

APPENDIX D

CRITICAL CRACK CALCULATIONS

It was assumed that the fuselage rupture and associated star-burst petalling process was driven by an expanding 'bubble' of high pressure gas, produced by the conversion of solid explosive material into gas products. As the explosive gas pressures reduced due to dissipation through the structure and external venting, the service differential pressure loading would have taken over from the explosive pressures as the principal force driving the skin fractures.

The high temperature gas would initially have been confined within the container where, because of the low volume, the pressure would have been extremely high (too high for containment) and the gas bubble would have expanded violently into the cavities of the fuselage between the outer skin and the container. This gas bubble would have continued to expand, with an accompanying fall in pressure due to the increasing volume combined with a corresponding drop in temperature.

The precise nature of the gas expansion process could not be determined directly from the evidence and it was therefore necessary to make a number of assumptions about its behaviour, based on the geometry of the hull and the area of fuselage skin which the high pressure bubble would have ruptured. Essentially, it was assumed that the gas bubble would expand freely in the circumferential direction, into the cavity between the fuselage skin and the container. In contrast, the freedom for the bubble to expand longitudinally would have been restricted by the presence of the fuselage frames, which would have partially blocked the passage of gas in the fore and aft directions. However, the pressures acting on the frames would have been such that they would have buckled and failed, allowing the gas to vent into the next 'bay', producing failure of the next frame. This sequential frame-failure process would have continued until the pressure had fallen to a level which the frames could withstand. During the period of frame failure and the associated longitudinal expansion of the gas bubble, this expansion rate was assumed to be half that of the circumferential rate.

It was assumed that venting would have taken place through the ruptured skin and that the boundary of the petalled hole followed behind the expanding gas bubble, just inside its outer boundary, i.e. the expanding gas bubble would have stretched and 'unzipped' the skins as it expanded. This process would have continued until the gas bubble had expanded/vented to a level where the pressure was no longer able to drive the petalling mechanism because the skin stresses had reduced to below the natural strength of the material.

The following structural model was assumed:

(i)   The pressurised hull was considered to be a cylinder of radius 128 inches, divided into regular lengths by stiff frames.

(ii)   The contributions of the stringers and frames beyond the petalled region were considered to be the equivalent of a reduction of stress in the skins by 20%, corresponding to an increase in skin thickness from 0.064 inches to 0.080 inches.

(iii)   Standing skin loads were assumed to be present due to the service differential pressure, i.e.. it was assumed that no significant venting of internal cabin pressure occurred within the relevant timescale.

(iv)   The mechanism of bubble pressure load transfer into the skins was:

     a. Hoop direction - conventional membrane reaction into hoop stresses.

     b. Longitudinal direction - reaction of pressures locally by the frames, restrained by the skins.

The critical crack calculations were based upon the generalised model of a plate under biaxial loading in which there was an elliptical hole with sharp cracks emanating from it. This is a good approximation of the initial condition, i.e.. the shattered hole, and an adequate representation of the subsequent phase, when the hole was enlarging in its star-burst, petalling, mode.

The analyses of critical crack dimensions in the circumferential and longitudinal directions were based on established Fracture Resistance techniques. The method utilises fracture resistance data for the material in question to establish the critical condition at which the rate of energy released by the crack just balances the rate of energy absorbed by the material in the cracking process, i.e. the instantaneous value of the parameter Kr, commonly referred to as the fracture toughness Kc.' From this, the relationship between critical stress and crack length can be determined.

Using conventional Linear Elastic Fracture Mechanics (LEFM) with fracture toughness data from RAE experimental work and published geometric factors relating to cracks emanating from elliptical holes, the stress levels required to drive cracks of increasing lengths in both circumferential and longitudinal directions were calculated. The skin stresses at sequential stages of the expanding gas bubble/skin petalling process were then calculated and compared with these data.

The results of the analysis indicated that, once the large petalled hole had been produced by explosive gas overpressure, the hoop stresses generated by fuselage pressurisation loads acting alone would have been sufficient to drive cracks longitudinally for large distances beyond the boundaries of the petalled hole. Thus, with residual gas overpressure acting as well, the 43 feet (total length) longitudinal fractures observed in the wreckage are entirely understandable. The calculations also suggested that the hoop fractures, due to longitudinal stresses in the skins, would have extended beyond the boundary of the petalled hole, though the excess stress driving the fractures in this direction would have been much smaller than for the longitudinal fractures, and the level of uncertainty was greater due to the difficulty of producing an accurate model reflecting the diffusion of longitudinal loads into the skins. Nevertheless, the results suggested that the circumferential cracks would extend downwards just beyond the keel, and upwards as far as the window belt - conclusions which accord reasonably well with the wreckage evidence.

APPENDIX E

POTENTIAL REMEDIAL MEASURES

1 . Introduction

In the following discussion, those damage mechanisms which appear to have contributed to the catastrophic structural failure of Flight PA103 are identified and possible ways of reducing their damaging effects are suggested. These suggestions are intended to stimulate thought and discussion by manufacturers, airworthiness authorities, and others having an interest in finding solutions to the problem; they are intended to serve as a catalyst rather than to lay claim to a definitive solution. On the basis of the Flight PA103 investigation, damage is likely to fall into two categories: direct explosive damage, and indirect explosive damage.

2. Direct explosive damage

The most serious aspect of the direct explosive damage on the structure is the large, jagged aperture in the pressure hull, combined with frame and stringer break-up, which results from the star-burst rupture of the fuselage skin. Because of its uncontrolled size and position, and the naturally radiating cracks which form as part of the petalling process, the skin's critical crack length (under pressurisation loading) is likely to be exceeded, resulting in unstable crack propagation away from the boundary of the aperture. Such cracks can lead to a critical loss of structural integrity at a time when additional loads are likely to be imposed on the structure due to reflected blast pressure and/or aircraft aerodynamic and inertial loading.

A further complicating factor is that the size of this aperture is likely to be sufficiently large to allow complete cargo containers and other debris to be ejected into the airstream, with a high probability of causing catastrophic structural damage to the empennage.

3 . Indirect explosive damage

Indirect explosive damage (channelling or ducting of explosive energy in the form of both shock waves and supersonic gas flows) is likely to occur because of the network of interlinked cavities which exist, in various forms, in all large commercial aircraft, particularly below cabin floor level. This channeling mechanism can produce critical damage at significant distances from the source of the explosion.

In addition to the structural damage, aircraft flight control and other critical systems will potentially be disrupted, both by the explosive forces and as a result of structural breakup and distortions. The discussion which follows focuses on possible means of limiting structural damage of the kind which occurred on Flight **PA** 103. Undoubtedly, such measures will also have beneficial effects in limiting systems damage. However, system vulnerability can further be reduced by applying, wherever possible, those techniques used on military aircraft to reduce vulnerability to battle damage; multiplexed, multiply redundant systems using distributed hardware to minimise risk of a single area of damage producing major system disruption. Fly by wire flight control systems potentially offer considerable scope to achieve these goals, but the same distributed approach would also **be** required for the electronic and other equipment which, in current aircraft, tends to be concentrated into a small number of 'equipment centres'.

4. Remedial measures to reduce structural damage

Whilst pure containment of the explosive energy is theoretically possible, in an aviation context such a scheme would not be viable. Any unsuccessful attempt to contain the explosive will probably produce greater devastation than the original (uncontained) explosion since all the explosive energy would merely be stored until the containment finally ruptured, when the stored energy would be released together with massive fragmentation of the containment.

However, a mixed approach involving a combination of containment, venting, and energy absorption should provide useful gains provided that a systematic rather than piecemeal approach is adopted, and that the scheme also addresses blast channelling. The following scheme is put forward for discussion, primarily as means of identifying, by example, how the various elements of the problem might be approached at a conceptual level and to provide a stimulus for debate. No detailed engineering solutions are offered, but it is firmly believed that the requirements of such a scheme could be met from a technical standpoint. The proposed scheme is based on the need to counter a threat similar to that involving Flight PA103, i.e. a high explosive device placed within a baggage container, however, the principles should be applicable to other aircraft types.

Such a scheme might comprise several 'layers' of defence. The first two layers, one within the other, are essentially identical and provide partial containment of the explosive energy and the redirection of blast out from the compartment via predetermined vent paths. Although the containment is temporary, it must provide an effective barrier to uncontrolled venting, preventing the escape of blast except via the pre-designated paths.

The third layer comprises a pre-determined area of fuselage skin, adjoining the outer end of the vent path, designed to rupture or burst in a controlled manner, providing a large vent aperture which will not tend to crack or rupture beyond the designated boundaries.

A fourth layer of protection has two elements, both intended to limit the propagation of shock waves through the internal cavities in the hull. The first element comprises the closure of any gaps between the vent apertures in the two innermost containment layers and the vent aperture in the outer skin. This effectively provides an exhaust duct connecting the inner and outer vent apertures to minimise leakage into the intervening structure and cavities around the cargo hold. The second element comprises the incorporation of an energy absorbing lining material within all the cavities in the lower hull, to absorb shock energy, limit shock reflection and limit the propagation of pressure waves which might enter the cavities, for example because of containment layer breakthrough.

5 Possible application to Boeing 747 type aircraft

5.1 Container Modification

The obvious candidates for the inner containment layer are the baggage containers themselves. Existing containers are of crude construction, typically comprising aluminium sheet sides and top attached to an aluminium frame with a fabric reinforced access curtain, or have sides and top of fibreglass laminate attached to a robust aluminium base section.

These containers are stacked in the aircraft in such a manner that on three sides (except for the endmost containers) the baggage within the adjoining containers provides an already highly effective energy absorbing barrier. If the container is modified so that loading access is via the outboard side of the container rather than at the end, i.e. the curtain is put on the faces shown in Figure E-1, then only the top and base are 'unbacked' by other containers, leaving the outboard face as a vent region.

The proposal is therefore that a modified container is developed in which the access is changed from the end to the outside face only, and which is modified to improve the resistance to internal pressures and thus encourage venting via the new access curtain only. How the container is actually modified to achieve the containment requirement is a matter of detail design, but two approaches suggest themselves, both involving the use of composite type materials. The first approach is to adopt a scheme for a rigid container which relies on a combination of energy absorption and burst strength to prevent uncontrolled breakout of explosive energy. The second approach is to use a 'flexible' container, i.e. rigid enough for normal use, but sufficiently flexible to allow gross deformation of shape without rupture. This, particularly if used with a backing blanket made from high performance material to resist fragmentation, could deform sufficiently to allow the container to bear against, and partially crush, adjoining containers. In this way, the shock energy transmission should be significantly reduced and the inherent energy absorption capability and mass of the baggage in adjoining containers could be utilised, whilst still retaining the high pressure gas for long enough to allow venting via the side face. Clearly, care would need to be taken to ensure that the container vent aperture remained as undistorted as possible, to ensure minimal leakage at the interface.

5.2 Cargo bay liner

The existing cargo bay liner is a thin fibreglass laminate which lines the roof and sidewalls of the cargo hold. There is no floor as such; instead, the containers are supported on rails running fore and aft on the tops of the fuselage frame lower segments. In a number of areas, there are zipped fabric panels let into the liner to provide access to equipment located behind. The liner 'ceiling' is suspended on plastic pillars approximately 2 centimeters below the bottom of the main cabin floor beams. The purpose of the liner is solely to act as a general barrier to protect wiring looms and systems components.

The proposal is to produce a new liner designed to provide the second level of containment, essentially at 'floor' and 'roof level only [Figure E-1]. The dimensional constraints are such that potentially quite thick material could be incorporated (leaving aside the weight problem), permitting not only a rigid liner design, but semi-rigid or flexible linings backed by energy absorbing blanket materials.

The liner would be designed to provide an additional barrier at the base and roof of the containers, which unlike the sides, are not protected by adjoining containers. The outside ends of these barrier elements must effectively seal against the vent apertures in the containers, to minimise leakage into the fuselage cavities.

5.3 Structural blow-out regions.

The final element in the containment/venting part of the scheme is a line of blow-out regions in the fuselage skins, coinciding exactly with the positions of the vent apertures in the cargo containers and cargo bay liner. These should extend along the length of the cargo hold, zoned in such a way that rupture due to rapid overpressure will occur in a controlled manner. The primary function of the blow-out regions would be to provide immediate pressure relief by allowing the inevitable skin rupture to take place only within pre-determined zones, limiting the extent of the skin tearing by means of careful stiffness control at the boundary of the blow-out regions.

The structural requirements of such panels are perhaps the most difficult challenge to meet, particularly for existing designs. However, it is believed that by giving appropriate consideration to the directionality of fastening strengths, and the use of external tear straps, it should be possible to design the structure to carry the normal service loads whilst creating a pre-disposition to rupturing in a controlled manner in response to gross pressure impulse loading.

The implementation of such features will need carefully balanced design in order to provide local stiffening, sufficient to control and direct the tear processes, without creating stiffness discontinuities which could lead to fatigue problems during extended service. However, the degree of reinforcement needed at the blow-out aperture need only be sufficient to limit tearing and to sustain the aircraft long enough to complete the flight unpressurised.

All aircraft have pre-existing strength discontinuities, despite the efforts of the designers to eliminate them. By choosing the positions of butt joints, lap joints, anti-tear straps and similar structural features in future designs, so as to incorporate them into the boundary of the blow-out panel region, the natural "tear here" tendencies of such features could possibly be turned to advantage. In the case of current generation aircraft, the positions of existing lines of weakness at such features will determine the optimum position for structural blow-out areas, and hence the positions of the container and cargo bay liner blow-out panels. A limited amount of local structural reinforcement (e.g. in the form of external anti-tear straps), carried out as part of a modification program, could perhaps fine tune the tearing properties of existing lines of weakness, potentially producing significant improvements.

5.4 Closure of cavities

There are four main classes of cavity which will need to be addressed on the Boeing 747, and most other modern aircraft. These are:

(i)   The channels formed between fuselage frames

(ii)   The cross-ship cavities between cabin floor beams

(iii)   Longitudinal 'manifold' cavities on each side of the cargo deck, running fore and aft in the space behind the upper sidewall areas of the cargo bay liner.

(iv)   Air conditioning vents along the bottom of the cabin side-liner panels, which connect the side cavities below cabin floor level with the main passenger cabin.

If the containment barriers (i.e. modified cargo containers and cargo hold liner) can be made to prevent blast breakthrough into these cavities directly, then the only area where transfer can occur is at the interface between the container/cargo hold liner vent apertures and the fuselage skins at the blow-out region. This short distance will need to be sealed in order to form a short 'exhaust duct' between the container vent aperture and the fuselage skin. Since the shock and general explosive pressure will act mainly along the vent-duct axis, the pressure loading on the vent duct walls should not be excessive.

5.5 Attenuation of shock waves in structural cavities

To prevent the 'ducting' of any blast which does enter the fuselage cavities, either because of partial penetration of the containment barriers or leakage at the vent duct interfaces, the scheme requires the provision of lightweight energy absorbing material within the cavities to limit reflection and propagation of pressure waves within the cavities, and radiation of shock waves into the cabin from the conditioning air vents. Materials such as vermiculite, which are of low density yet have excellent explosive energy absorption properties, may have application in this area, perhaps in lieu of the existing insulation material.

Since the existing cavities often serve as part of the air conditioning outflow circuit, some consideration will need to be given to finding an alternative route. However, the flow rates are small compared with the total cross-sectional flow potential of the cavities and this function could be served by separate air conditioning ducts, or perhaps by restricting access to one or two cavities only (thus limiting the risk), or by using some form of blast valve to close off the air conditioning vents. Similarly, the requirement to vent pressure from the cabin in the event of a cargo bay decompression would also need to be addressed.

189

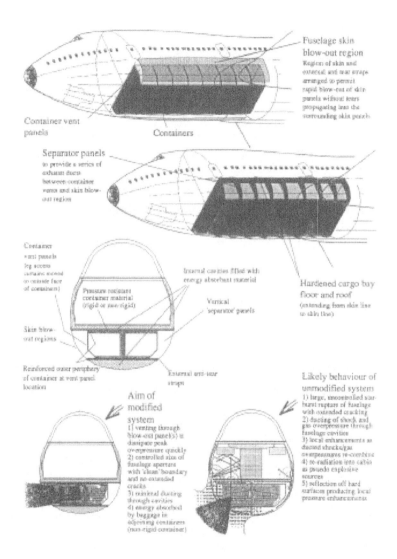

Principal Features of Proposed Remedial Scheme

Figure E-1

APPENDIX F

BAGAGE CONTAINER EXAMINATION AND RECONSTRACTION

1. Introduction

During the wreckage recovery operation it became apparent that some items, identified as parts of baggage containers, exhibited blast damage. It was confirmed by forensic scientists at the Royal Armaments Research and Development Establishment (RARDE), after detailed physical and chemical examination, that these items showed conclusive evidence of a detonating high performance plastic explosive. It was therefore decided to segregate identifiable container parts and reconstruct any that showed evidence from the effect of Improvised Explosive Device (TED). It was evident, from the main wreckage layout that the IED had been located in the forward cargo hold and, although all baggage container wreckage was examined, only items from the forward hold showing the relevant characteristics were considered for the reconstruction. This Appendix documents the reconstruction of two particular containers and, from their position within the forward fuselage, defines the location of the IED.

2 Container Arrangement

Information supplied by Pan Am showed that this aircraft had been loaded with 12 baggage containers and two cargo pallets in the forward hold located as shown in Figure F-1. Three containers were recorded as being of the glass fibre reinforced plastic type (those at positions 11L, 13L and 21L) with the remaining 9 being of metal construction.

3. Container Description

All the baggage containers installed in the forward cargo hold were of the LD3 type (lower deck container, half width - cargo) and designated with the codes AVE, for those constructed from aluminum alloy, and AVA or AVN for those constructed from fibreglass. Each container was specifically identified with a four digit serial number followed by the letters PA and this nine digit identifier was present at the top of three sides of each container in black letters/numbers approximately 5 inches tall. Detail drawings and photographs of a typical metal container are shown in Figure F-2. Each container was essentially a 5 feet cube with a 17 inch extension over its full length to the left of the access aperture. In order to fit within the section of the lower fuselage this extension had a sloping face at its base joining the edge of the container floor to the left vertical sidewall at a position some 20 inches above the floor. The access aperture on the AVE type container was covered by a blue reinforced plastic curtain, fixed to the container at its top edge, braced by two wires and central and lower edge cross bars which engaged with the aperture structure. The strength of this type of container superstructure was provided by the various extruded section edge members, attached to a robust floor panel, with a thin aluminum skin providing baggage containment and weatherproofing.

4. Container Identification

Discrimination between forward and rear cargo hold containers was relatively straightforward as the rear cargo hold wreckage was almost entirely confined to the town of Lockerbie and was characteristically different from that from the forward hold, in that it was generally severely crushed and covered in mud. The forward hold debris, by comparison, was mostly recovered from the southern wreckage trail some distance from Lockerbie and had mainly been torn into relatively large sections.

All immediately identifiable parts of the forward cargo containers were segregated into areas designated by their serial numbers and items not identified at that stage were collected into piles of similar parts for later assessment. As a result of this two containers, one metal and one fibreglass, were identified as exhibiting damage likely to have been caused by the IED. From the Pan Am records the metal container of these two had been positioned at position 14L, and the fibreglass at position 21L (adjacent positions, 4th and 5th from the front of the forward cargo hold on the left side). The serial numbers of these containers were respectively AVE 4041 PA and AVN 7511 PA.

6. Container Reconstruction

Those parts which could be positively identified as being from containers AVE 4041 PA and AVN 7511 PA were assembled onto one of three wooden frameworks; one each for the floor and superstructure of container 4041, and one for the superstructure of container 7511. Figures F-3 to F-9 show the reconstruction of container 4041 and Figure F-10 shows the reconstructed forward face of container 7511. Approximately 85% of container 4041 was identified, the main missing sections being the aft half of the sloping face skin and all of the curtain. Two items were included which could not be fracture or tear matched to container 4041, however, they showed the particular type of blast damage exhibited only by items from this container.

While this work was in progress a buckled section of skin from container 4041 was found by an AAIB Inspector to contain, trapped within its folds, an item which was subsequently identified by forensic scientists at the Royal Armaments Research and Development Establishment (RARDE) as belonging to a specific type of radio-cassette player and that this had been fitted with an improvised explosive device. Examination of all other component parts of the remaining containers from the front and rear cargo holds did not reveal any evidence of blast damage similar to that found on containers 4041 and 7511.

Those items which were positively identified as parts of container 4041 or 7511, and for which a grid reference was available, were found to have fallen close to the southern edge of the southern wreckage trail. This indicated that one of the very early events in the aircraft break-up sequence was the blast damage to, and ejection of, parts of these two containers.

In order to gain a better understanding of the failure sequence, that part of the aircraft's fuselage encompassing the forward cargo hold was reconstructed at AAIB Farnborough. After all available blast damaged pieces of structure had been added, the floor of container 4041 was installed as near to its original position as the deformation of the wreckage would allow and this is shown in Figure F-11. The presence of this floor panel in the fuselage greatly assisted the three-dimensional assessment of the 1ED location. Witness marks between this floor and the aircraft structure, tie down rail, roller rail and relative areas of blast damage left no doubt that container 4041 had been located at position 14L at the time of detonation.

7. Analysis

The general character of damage that could be seen on the reconstructions of containers 4041 and 7511 was not of a type seen on the wreckage of any of the other containers examined. In particular, the reconstruction of the floor of container 4041 revealed an area of severe distortion, tearing and blackening localised in its aft outboard quarter which, together with the results of the forensic examination of items from this part of the container, left no doubt that the LED had detonated within this container.

Within container 4041 the lack of direct blast damage (of the type seen on the outboard floor edge member and lower portions of the aft face structural members) on most of the floor panel in the heavily distorted area suggested that this had been protected by, presumably, a piece of luggage. The downward heaving of the floor in this area was sufficient to stretch the floor material, far enough to be cut by cargo bay sub structure, and distort the adjacent fuselage frames. This supported the view that the item of baggage containing the 1ED had been positioned fairly close to the floor but not actually placed upon it. The installation of the floor of container 4041 into the fuselage reconstruction (Figure F-11) showed the blast to have been centered almost directly above frame 700 and that its main effects had not only been directed mostly downwards and outboard but also rearwards. The blast effects on the aircraft skin were onto stringer 39L but centered at station 710 (Figure F-12). Downwards crushing at the top, and rearwards distortion of frame 700 was apparent as well as rearwards distortion of frame 720.

With the two container reconstructions placed together it became apparent that a relatively mild blast had exited container 4041 through the rear lower face to the left of the curtain and impinged at an angle on the forward face of container 7511. This had punched a hole, Figure F-10, approximately 8 inches square some 10 inches up from its base and removed the surface of this face inboard from the hole for some 50 inches. Radiating out from the hole were areas of sooting, and other black deposits, extending to the top of the container. No signs were present of any similar damage on other external or internal faces of container 7511 or the immediately adjacent containers 14R and 21R.

The above assessment of the directions of distortion, comparison of damage to both containers, and the related airframe damage adjacent to the container position, enabled the most probable lateral and vertical location of the lED to be established as shown in Figure F-13, centered longitudinally on station 700.

8. Conclusions

Throughout the general examination of the aircraft wreckage, direct evidence of blast damage was exhibited on the airframe only in the area bounded, approximately, by stations 700 and 720 and stringers 38L and 40L. Blast damage was found only on pieces of containers 4042 and 7511, the relative location and character of which left no doubt that it was directly associated with airframe damage. Thus, these two containers had been loaded in positions 14L and 21L as recorded on the Pan Am cargo loading documents. There was also no doubt that the 1ED had been located within container 14L, specifically in its aft outboard quarter as indicated in Figure F-13, centered on station 700.

195

Blast damage to the forward face of container 7511 was as a direct result of hot gases/fragments escaping from the aft face of container 4041. No evidence was seen to suggest that more than one 1ED had detonated on Flight PA 103

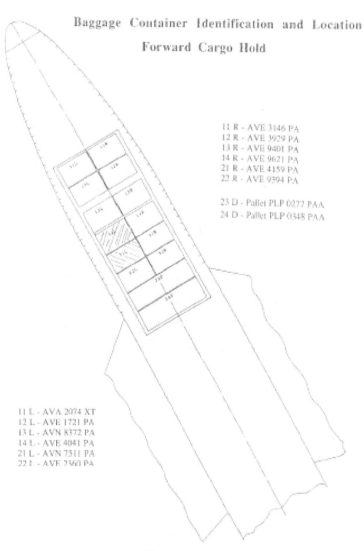

Baggage Container Identification and Location

Forward Cargo Hold

11 R - AVE 3146 PA
12 R - AVE 3929 PA
13 R - AVE 9401 PA
14 R - AVE 9621 PA
21 R - AVE 4159 PA
22 R - AVE 9394 PA

23 D - Pallet PLP 0277 PAA
24 D - Pallet PLP 0348 PAA

11 L - AVA 2074 XT
12 L - AVE 1721 PA
13 L - AVN 8372 PA
14 L - AVE 4041 PA
21 L - AVN 7511 PA
22 L - AVE 2361 PA

Figure F-1

PAN AM DATA (6) CODE ... AKE
OTHER CODES ... LD3

RATE CLASSIFICATION
  International ... 8
  US Domestic ... LD3

MAXIMUM GROSS WEIGHT (INCLUDES TARE)
  3500 lb   1588 kg

TARE
  240 ± 20 lb   109 ± 9 kg
  Weight varies. Check weight on unit.

USABLE INTERIOR VOLUME
  139 cu ft   4 cu m

DIMENSIONS	INCHES	CENTIMETERS
Base Size	61 D x 62 W	153 D x 156 W
Maximum Height	64 H	163 H
Maximum Door Opening	57 W x 62 H	145 W x 157 H

• All dimensions and weights rounded off to nearest whole number.
• Inside dimensions are 3 to 7 inches (8 to 15 cm) less than base and maximum height.

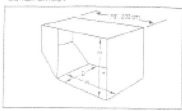

Lower Deck Container
Half Width—Cargo

Figure F-2

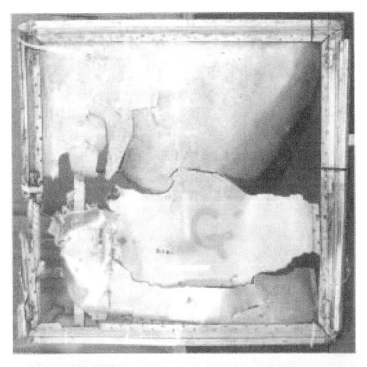

Detail of Damage to Container Floor

Figure F-3

BAGGAGE CONTAINER FLOOR DAMAGE DIAGRAM

FWD

↑

APPROXIMATE LIMIT OF FLOOR DISTORTION DUE TO BLAST
EFFECTS

← OUTBOARD

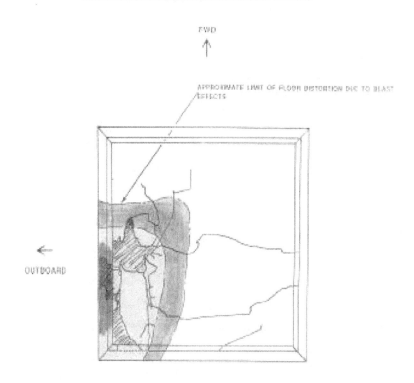

N739PA - FLOOR PANEL MAP FROM CONTAINER

AREA OF INTENSE DISTORTION, INFLUENCED BY AIRCRAFT
STRUCTURE UNDER PANEL

TEAR LINES

EDGE MEMBER SEVERELY BLAST DAMAGED OVER THIS AREA —

AREAS NOT RECOVERED

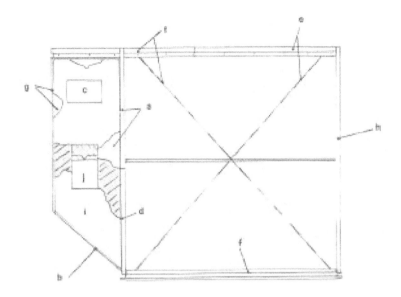

a   Curtain apperture left side vertical edge member, upper half

b   Sloping face edge member

c   Container manufacturer's data plate containing burnt piece of material which itself contained a fragment of circuit board

d   Curtain apperture left side vertical edge member, lower half

e   Upper edge member, right half, attached to roof edge member and one curtain bar

f   Upper edge member, left half, attached to roof edge member, curtain wire and lower curtain bar

g   Left edge vertical member

h   Curtain apperture right side vertical member

i   Left side lower skin section adjoining sloping face

j   Soot stained plastic sheet

Aft face of container AVE 4041 PA, view looking forward

Figure F-5

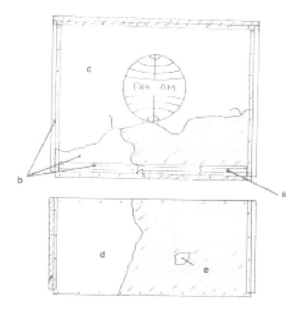

a   Stiffener section from
    base of vertical face

b   Vertical face forward
    edge member, lower
    stiffener section and
    skin fragment

c   Distorted upper section
    of vertical face skin

d   Forward section of
    sloping face skin,
    severely distorted

e   Fragment of container
    skin, provisionally
    thought to be part
    of sloping face skin.

Outboard faces of AVE 4041

Figure F-6

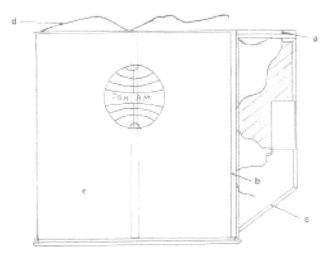

a   Outboard section of roof edge member

b   Forward face outboard skin, attached to vertical edge member

c   Forward edge member of sloping face

d   Roof skin panel, complete except for aft outboard corner

e   Forward face panel, complete with top, left and lower edge members

Forward face of AVE 4041 PA
Figure F-7

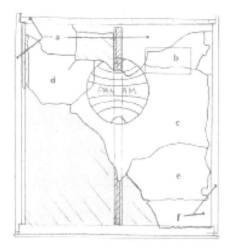

a Aft, top and roof edge members including upper section of skin

b Repair patch from upper right side

c Mid section of skin including stiffener section

d Upper skin section

e Lower skin section

f Right side vertical edge member attached to lower piece of skin

Inboard face of container AVE 4041 PA

Figure F-8

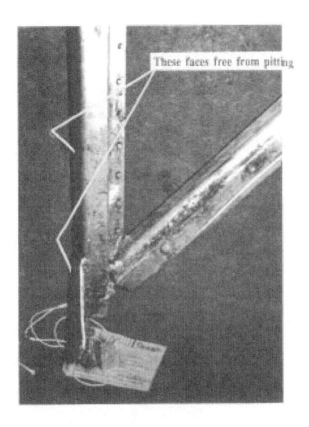

These faces free from pitting

Detail of items from aft face of container
AVE 4041 PA showing evidence of blast
damage

Figure F-9

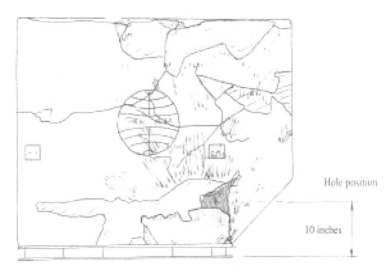

Hole position

10 inches

Forward face of container AVN 7511 PA,
view looking aft

Figure F-10

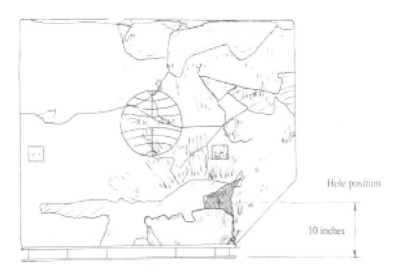

Hole position

10 inches

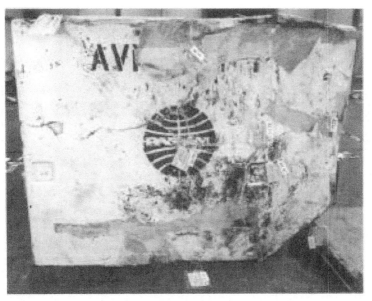

Forward face of container AVN 7511 PA,
view looking aft

Figure F-10

206

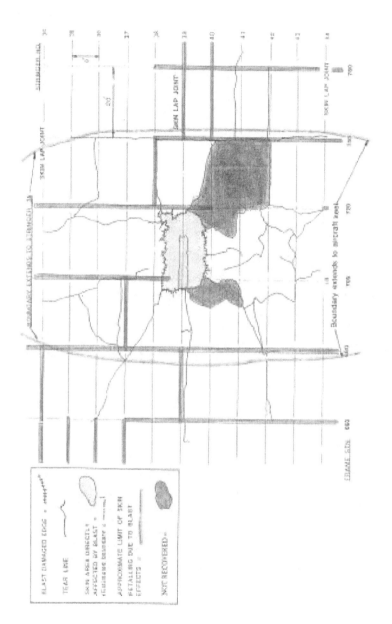

N739PA Skin Structure Damage Diagram

Figure F-12

207

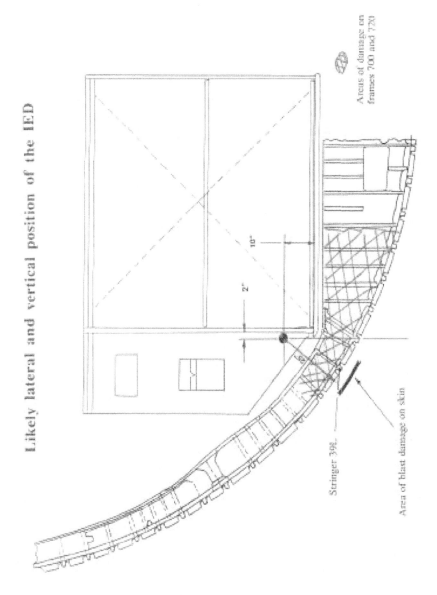

Figure F-13

APPENDIX G

MACH STEM SHOCK WAVE EFFECTS

1 . Introduction

An explosive detonation within a fuselage, in reasonably close proximity to the skin, will produce a high intensity shock wave which will propagate outwards from the centre of detonation. On reaching the inner surface of the fuselage skin, energy will partially be absorbed in shattering, deforming and accelerating the skin and stringer material in its path. Much of the remaining energy will be transmitted, as a shock wave, through the skin and into the atmosphere but a significant amount of energy will be returned as a reflected shock wave, which will travel back into the fuselage interior where it will interact with the incident shock to produce Mach stem shocks - recombination shock waves which can have pressures and velocities of propagation greater than the incident shock.

The Mach stem phenomenon is significant for two reasons. Firstly, it gives rise (for relatively small charge sizes) to a geometric limitation on the area of skin material which the incident shock wave can shatter. This geometric limitation occurs irrespective of charge size (within the range of charge sizes considered realistic for the Flight PA103 scenario), and thus provides a means of calculating the standoff distance of the explosive charge from the fuselage skin. Secondly, the Mach stem may have been a significant factor in transmitting explosive energy through the fuselage cavities, producing damage at a number of separate sites remote from the source of the explosion.

2. Mach stem shock wave formation

A Mach stem shock is formed by the interaction between the incident and reflected shock waves, resulting in a coalescing of the two waves to produce a new, single, shock wave. If an explosive charge is detonated in a free field at some standoff distance from a reflective surface, then the incident shock wave expands spherically until the wave front contacts the reflective surface, when that element of the wave surface will be reflected back (Figure G-1). The local angle between the spherical wave front and the reflecting surface is zero at the point where the reflecting surface intersects the normal axis, resulting in wave reflection directly back towards the source and maximum reflected overpressure at the reflective surface. The angle between the wave front and the reflecting surface at other locations increases with distance from the normal axis, producing a corresponding increase in the oblique angle of reflection of the wave element, with a corresponding reduction in the reflected overpressure. (To a first order of approximation, explosive shock waves can be considered to follow similar reflection and refraction paths to light waves, ref: "Geometric Shock Initiation of Pyrotechnics and Explosives", R Weinheimer, McDonnel Douglas Aerospace Co.) Beyond some critical (conical) angle about the normal axis, typically around 40 degrees, the reflected and incident waves coalesce to form Mach stem shock waves which, effectively, bisect the angle between the incident and reflected waves, and thus travel approximately at right angles to the normal axis, i.e.parallel with the reflective surface (detail "A", figure G-1).

3. Estimation of charge standoff distance from the fuselage skin

Within the constraint of the likely charge size used on Flight PA103, calculations suggested that the initial Mach stem shock wave pressure close to the region of Mach stem formation (i.e. the shock wave *face-on* pressure, acting at right angles to the skin), was likely to be more than twice that of the incident shock wave, with a velocity of propagation perhaps 25% greater. However, the Mach stem out-of-plane pressure, i.e.the pressure felt by the reflecting surface where the Mach stem touches it, would have been relatively low and insufficient to shatter the skin material. Therefore, provided that the charge had sufficient energy to produce skin shatter within the conical central region where no Mach stems form, the size of the shattered region would be a function mainly of charge standoff distance, and charge weight would have had little influence. Consequently, it was possible to calculate the charge standoff distance required to produce a given size of shattered skin from geometric considerations alone. On this basis, a charge standoff distance of approximately 25 to 27 inches would have resulted in a shattered region of some 18 to 20 inches in diameter, broadly comparable to the size of the shattered region evident on the three-dimensional wreckage reconstruction.

Whilst the analytical method makes no allowance for the effect of the IED casing, or any other baggage or container structure interposed between the charge and the fuselage skin, the presence of such a barrier would have tended to absorb energy rather than redirect the transmitted shock wave; therefore its presence would have been more critical in terms of charge size than of position. Certainly, the standoff distance predicted by this method was strikingly similar to the figure of 25 inches derived independently from the container and fuselage reconstructions

212

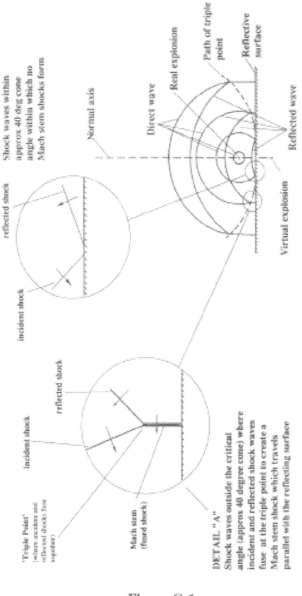

Figure G-1

Mach Stem Shock Formation

Prepared from CRC supplied by the Department

Printed in the United Kingdom for HMSO.
Dd.293152, 8/98, C25, 33963, 5672, (1765).

IN THE AFTERMATH...

Editor's Note

It is not the purpose of this book to develop any new theory on the bombing of PANAM Flight 103, nor to judge all the things that have happened, written or said over the issue since that fatal date of 21 December 1988. In a "normal" aviation accident the plausible cause, if any, is the start of an improvement in the aviation systems.

In this case there was a breach of security. Aviation security is in todays world unfortunately a key issue of the system. The investigation of this breach was not a part of the British Air Accidents Investigation Branch, the entity that investigated the accident. As said before aviation security is a key issue of the aviation system, the story would therefore not be complete if no attention is paid to what happened after the accident.

Numerous books and articles, movies and documentaries have been written or made over the bombing of PANAM Flight 103. There were cases in court, millions of dollars have been paid to informers and other interesting parties that had something to do with the issue. One man was eventually convicted, but later, against the wishes of the USA, released from jail by the Scottish authorities, on compassionate grounds. What follows is a summary of the highlights.

The Main Issue

It took only a few days to find out that PANAM Flight 103 was brought down by a bomb. A bomb as such has nothing to do with aviation, but a bomb on board an airplane is a different matter. There are two reasons why it was of the utmost importance to find out what had happened:

    1.   How did the bomb came on board PANAM Flight 103?

    2.   Who was behind it?

Both questions were important in order to prevent repetition, certainly if one takes into account the fact that in 1988 tight airport and aviation security was supposed to be in place. Only a few years earlier Air India Flight 182 was brought down over the Atlantic Ocean by a bomb, killing 329. Airport security failed to detect the bomb.

The investigation into the bombing of Pan Am Flight 103

The investigation began at 19:03 on December 21, 1988 when Pan Am Flight 103 was blown up over Lockerbie in Dumfries and Galloway, Scotland. Lockerbie is located about 20 kilometres northeast of the town of Dumfries on the west coast of Scotland.

In Scotland, responsibility for the investigation of sudden deaths rests with the local *Procurator Fiscal* (public prosecutor), who attends the scene and may direct the police in the conduct of their inquiries. The Procurator Fiscal holds a commission from *His Majesty's Advocate* (the Lord Advocate), who is Scotland's chief law officer. Responsibility for the Lockerbie investigation thus rested with Jimmy McDougall, the Procurator Fiscal in the nearby town of *Dumfries*, the smallest police force by number of officers in the United Kingdom. The police effort was therefore augmented by officers from all over Scotland as well as the north of England, and the Procurator Fiscal was given support from the *Crown Office and Procurator Fiscal Service* in Edinburgh. Funding the investigation quickly became a political issue and Margaret Thatcher (England's Prime Minister at that time) announced that *central government*, not the *Scottish Office*, would meet any additional costs involved.

War Zone

The small town of Lockerbie, hardly 4.000 inhabitants, did look like a war zone. On the ground, 11 Lockerbie residents were killed when the wing section hit 13 Sherwood Crescent at more than 800 km/h (500 mph) and exploded, creating a crater 47 m (154 ft) long and with a volume of 560 m^3 (730 cu yd), vaporizing the house and its occupants, Dora and Maurice Henry. Several other houses and their foundations were completely destroyed, and 21 others were damaged so badly they had to be demolished. Four members of one family, Jack and Rosalind Somerville and their children Paul and Lynsey, died when their house at 15 Sherwood Crescent exploded.

Kathleen Flannigan, age 41, Thomas Flannigan, 44, and their daughter Joanne, 10, were killed by the explosion in their house 16 Sherwood Crescent. Their son Steven, 14, saw the fireball engulf his home from a neighbour's garage where he had gone to repair his sister's bicycle.

The fireball rose above the houses and moved toward the nearby *Glasgow–Carlisle A74* dual carriageway, scorching cars in the southbound lanes and leading motorists and local residents to believe that there had been a meltdown at the nearby *Chapelcross nuclear power station*. Father Patrick Keegans, Lockerbie's Roman Catholic priest, was preparing to visit his neighbours at around 7 p.m. that evening when the plane destroyed their home. There was nothing left of them to bury. The priest's home, at 1 Sherwood Crescent, was the only house that was neither destroyed by the impact or gutted by fire.

For many days, Lockerbie residents lived with the sight of bodies in their gardens and in the streets, as forensic workers photographed and tagged the location of each body to help determine the exact position and force of the on-board explosion, by coordinating information about each passenger's assigned seat, type of injury, and where they had landed.

On December 28, 1988, just a week after the crash, the Air Accidents Investigation Branch announced that they had found traces of high explosives and that there was evidence that Pan Am 103 had been brought down by an *improvised explosive device* (IED). Over a thousand police officers and soldiers carried out fingertip searches of the crash site that lasted for months, retrieving more than 10,000 items from the fields and forests of southern Scotland. They were asked to look out particularly for items which might be charred and which might therefore have been close to an explosion.

An analysis by the American Federal Bureau of Investigation (FBI) and DERA forensic teams indicated that a chemical explosion had occurred; that a 12-ounce (340 g) to 16-ounce (450 g) charge of plastic explosive had been used; and that the device had exploded 8-inch (200 mm) from the left side of the container. DERA's Feraday and Dr. Thomas Hayes examined two strips of metal and found traces of pentaerythritol tetranitrate (PETN) and cyclotrimethylene trinitramine (RDX), components of Semtex-H, a high-performance plastic explosive manufactured in the village of Semtin, Czech Republic. In March 1990, Czechoslovakian President Václav Havel disclosed that the former communist regime had supplied a large consignment of Semtex via a company called Omnipol to the government of Libya.

During the fingertip searches around Lockerbie, 56 fragments of a suitcase were found that showed extensive, close-range blast damage. With the help of luggage manufacturers, it was determined that the fragments had been part of a brown, hardshell, Samsonite suitcase of the 26-inch (660 mm) Silhouette 4000 range. A further 24 items of luggage, including clothing, were determined by DERA (Britain's *Defence Evaluation and Research Agency*) to have been within a very close range of the suitcase when it exploded, and probably inside it.

The blast fragments included parts of a radio cassette player and a small piece of circuit board. This rang alarm bells within the intelligence communities in Britain, the U.S., and West Germany, as the West German police had recovered a Semtex bomb hidden inside a Toshiba radio cassette player in an apartment in Neuss, West Germany in October 1988, two months before PA 103 exploded. The bomb, one of five, had been in the possession of members of the Damascus–based *Popular Front for the Liberation of*

Palestine-General Command (PFLP-GC), led by Ahmed Jibril, a former Syrian army captain. DERA's Alan Feraday travelled to West Germany to examine this bomb, and though he found that the Lockerbie fragments did not precisely match the Toshiba model, but they were similar enough for him to contact Toshiba. With the company's help, DERA discovered there were seven models in which the printed circuit board bore exactly the same details as the Lockerbie fragments.

Further examination of the clothing believed to have been in the bomb suitcase found fragments of paper (from a booklet on the Toshiba RT-SF 16 Bombeat radio cassette player) embedded into two Slalom-brand men's shirts, a blue baby's jumpsuit of the Babygro Primark brand, and a pair of tartan trousers. Fragments of plastic consistent with the material used on a Bombeat and pieces of loudspeaker mesh, were found embedded in other clothing which appeared to have been inside the bomb suitcase: a white, Abanderado-brand T-shirt; cream-coloured pyjamas; a fragment of a knitted, brown, woollen cardigan with the label "Puccini design"; a herringbone jacket; and brown herringbone material, some of which bore a label indicating it came from a pair of size-34 Yorkie-brand men's trousers.

Who was behind the bombing of PANAM Flight 103?

From the very beginning, actually even before the official investigation started, the air was full of rumours about possible perpetrators. Some theories were a result of the investigation, others were presented by third parties.

Helsinki warning

First there was the Helsinki warning. On 5 December 1988 the *Federal Aviation Administration* (FAA) issued a security bulletin saying that on that day a man with an Arabic accent had telephoned the U.S. Embassy in *Helsinki*, Finland, and had told them that a Pan Am flight from *Frankfurt* to the United States would be blown up within the next two weeks by someone associated with the *Abu Nidal Organization*. He said a Finnish woman would carry the bomb on board as an unwitting courier.

The anonymous warning was taken seriously by the U.S. government. The *State Department* cabled the bulletin to dozens of embassies. The FAA sent it to all U.S. carriers, including Pan Am, which had charged each of the passengers a $5 security surcharge, promising a "program that will screen passengers, employees, airport facilities, baggage and aircraft with unrelenting thoroughness" (*The Independent*, 29 March 1990); **the security team in Frankfurt found the warning hidden under a pile of papers on a desk the day after the bombing.** One of the Frankfurt security screeners, whose job it was to spot explosive devices under X-ray, told *ABC News* that she had first learned what *Semtex* (a plastic explosive) was during her ABC interview 11 months *after* the bombing (*Prime Time Live*, November 1989).

On 13 December, the warning was posted on bulletin boards in the U.S. Embassy in Moscow and eventually distributed to the entire American community there, including journalists and businessmen. As a result, a number of people allegedly booked on carriers other than Pan Am, leaving empty seats on PA103 that were later sold cheaply in "*bucket shops*".

PLO warning

Just days before the sabotage of the aircraft, security forces in a number of European countries, including Britain, were put on alert after a warning from the *Palestine Liberation Organization* (PLO) that extremists might launch terrorist attacks to undermine the then ongoing dialogue between the United States and the PLO.

Claims of responsibility

According to a CIA analysis dated 22 December 1988, several groups were quick to claim responsibility in telephone calls in the United States and Europe:

- A male caller claimed that a group called the *Guardians of the Islamic Revolution* had destroyed the plane in retaliation for the U.S. shootdown of *Iran Air Flight 655* in the Persian Gulf the previous July.

- A caller claiming to represent the *Islamic Jihad* organization told ABC News in New York that the group had planted the bomb.

- The *Ulster Defence Association* allegedly issued a telephone claim, apparently its first political move in 80 years, and probably came about from a demand from MI5 that the *PIRA (Provisional Irish Army)*, who have never used air terrorism not be implicated.

After finishing this list, the author stated, *"We consider the claims from the Guardians of the Islamic Revolution as the most credible one received so far"*. The analysis concluded, *"We cannot assign responsibility for this tragedy to any terrorist group at this time. We anticipate that, as often happens, many groups will seek to claim credit"*.

Popular Front for the Liberation of Palestine - General Command (PFLP-GC),

For many months after the bombing, the prime suspects were the *Popular Front for the Liberation of Palestine - General Command (PFLP-GC)*, a Damascus-based rejectionist group led by former Syrian army captain *Ahmed Jibril*, sponsored by Iran. In a February 1986 press conference, Jibril warned:

> "There will be no safety for any traveler on an Israeli or U.S. airliner" (*Cox and Foster* 1991, p28).

Secret intercepts were reported by author, *David Yallop*, to have recorded the *Iranian Revolutionary Guards (Pasdaran)* in *Baalbeck, Lebanon* making contact with the PFLP-GC immediately after the downing of the Iran Air Airbus. *Israeli intelligence* allegedly intercepted a telephone call made two days after PA 103 by *Mohtashemi-Pur*, Interior Minister in *Tehran*, to the *chargé d'affaires* at the Iranian embassy in *Beirut*, instructing the embassy to hand over the funds to Jibril and congratulating them on the success of operation 'Intekam' ('equal and just revenge'). Jibril is alleged to have received $11 million from Iran - although a banking *audit trail* to confirm the payment has never been presented.

Jibril's right hand man, *Hafez Dalkamoni*, set up a PFLP-GC cell which was active in the *Frankfurt* and *Neuss* areas of West Germany in October 1988, two months before PA 103. During what Germany's internal security service, the *Bundesamt für Verfassungsschutz* (BfV), called *Operation Herbstlaub* (Operation "Autumn Leaves"), the BfV kept cell members under strict surveillance. The plotters prepared a number of *improvised explosive devices* (IEDs) hidden inside household electronic equipment. They discussed a planned operation in coded calls to *Cyprus* and *Damascus:* "oranges and apples" stood for detonating devices; "medicine and pasta" for *Semtex* explosive; and, "auntie" for the bomb carrier. One operative had been recorded as saying: "auntie should get off, but should leave the suitcase on the bus" (*Duffy and Emerson* 1990). The PFLP-GC cell had an experienced bomb-maker, Jordanian *Marwan Khreesat*, to assist them. Khreesat made at least one IED inside a single-speaker Toshiba Bombeat 453 radio cassette recorder, similar to the twin speaker model RT-SF 16 Bombeat that was used to blow up PA 103. However, unlike the Lockerbie bomb with its sophisticated timer, Khreesat's IEDs contained a barometric pressure device that triggers a simple timer with a range of up to 45 minutes before detonation.

Unbeknown to the PFLP-GC cell, its bomb-maker Khreesat was a *Jordanian* intelligence service (GID) agent and reported on the cell's activities to the GID, who relayed the information to Western intelligence and to the BfV. The Jordanians encouraged Khreesat to make the bombs but instructed him to ensure they were ineffective and would not explode. (A German police technician would however be killed, in April 1989, when trying to disarm one of

Khreesat's IEDs). Through Khreesat and the GID, the Germans learned that the cell was surveying a number of targets, including Iberia Flight 888 from Madrid to Tel Aviv via Barcelona, chosen because the bomb-courier could disembark without baggage at Barcelona leaving the barometric trigger to activate the IED on the next leg of the journey. The date chosen, Khreesat reportedly told his handlers, was 30 October 1988. He also told them that two members of the cell had been to Frankfurt airport to pick up Pan Am timetables.

Acting upon this intelligence, the German secret police moved in to arrest the PFLP-GC cell on 26 October, raiding 14 apartments and arresting 17 men, fearing that to keep them under surveillance much longer was to risk losing control of the situation. Two cell members are known to have escaped arrest including *Abu Elias*, a resident of Sweden who, according to *Prime Time Live* (*ABC News* November 1989), was an expert in bombs sent to Germany to check on Khreesat's devices because of suspicions raised by Ahmed Jibril. Four IEDs were recovered, but Khreesat stated later that a fifth device had been taken away by Dalkamoni before the raid, and was never recovered. The link to PA 103 was further strengthened when Khreesat told investigators that, before joining the cell in Germany, he had bought five Toshiba Bombeat cassette radios from a smugglers' village in Syria close to the border with Lebanon, and made practice IEDs out of them in Jibril's training camp 20 km (12 miles) away. The bombs were inspected by Abu Elias, who declared them to be good work. What became of these devices is not known.

Some journalists believed that it was too stark a coincidence for a Toshiba cassette radio IED to have downed PA 103 just eight weeks after the arrest of the PFLP-GC cell in Frankfurt. Indeed, Scottish police actually wrote up an arrest warrant for Marwan Khreesat in the spring of 1989, but were persuaded by the FBI not to issue it because of his value as an intelligence source. In the following spring, King Hussein of Jordan arranged for Khreesat to be interviewed by FBI agent, Edward Marshman, and the former head of the FBI's forensic lab, Thomas Thurman, to whom he described in detail the bombs he had built. The author David Yallop speculated that Libyan and Iranian-paid agents may have worked on the bombing together; or, that one group handed the job over to a second group upon the arrest of the PFLP-GC cell members. The former CIA head of counter-terrorism, Vincent Cannistraro, who previously worked on the PA 103 investigation, in an interview said he believed the PFLP-GC planned the attack at the behest of the Iranian government, then sub-contracted it to Libyan intelligence after October 1988, because the arrests in Germany meant the PFLP-GC was unable to complete the operation. Other supporters of this theory believed that whoever paid for the bombing arranged two parallel operations intended to ensure that at least one would succeed; or, that Jibril's cell in Germany was a red herring designed to attract the attention of the intelligence services, while the real bombers worked quietly elsewhere.

Iran

A number of people considered that the Iranian revenge motive, retaliation for the shooting down of the Iran Air Airbus by USS *Vincennes* on 3 July 1988, killing 290 people, was prematurely dismissed by investigators. They drew attention to a comment by former British prime minister Margaret Thatcher in her 1993 memoirs, where she seemed to discount the Libya revenge motive (for the 1986 bombing of Tripoli and Benghazi by the United States air force):

> "It turned out to be a more decisive blow against Libyan-sponsored terrorism than I could ever have imagined. ...There were revenge killings of British hostages organized by Libya, which I bitterly regretted. But the much-vaunted Libyan counter attack did not and could not take place... There was a marked decline in Libyan-sponsored terrorism in succeeding years" (*Thatcher* 1993, pp448-9).

Additionally, *Abolghasem Mesbahi*, former head of Iranian intelligence in Europe, eventually defected and "told [German] investigators that

Iran had asked Libya and Abu Nidal, a Palestinian guerrilla leader, to carry out the attack on Pan Am 103."

The US *Defense Intelligence Agency* alleges that *Ali Akbar Mohtashamipur* (*Ayatollah Mohtashemi*), a member of the Iranian government, paid US$ 10 million for the bombing:

> *Ayatollah Mohtashemi: (...) and was the one who paid the same amount to bomb Pan Am Flight 103 in retaliation for the US shoot-down of the Iranian Airbus.*

Part of report, which is dated 1989-09-24, cites information acquired at *Ft. Meade, MD*:

> *The mission was to blow up a Pan Am flight that was to be almost entirely booked by US military personnel on Christmas leave. The flight was supposed to be a direct flight from Frankfurt, GE, to New York, not Pan Am flight 103 which was routed through London, UK. The suitcase containing the bomb was labeled with the name of one of the US passengers on the plane and was inadvertently placed on the wrong plane possibly by airport ground crew members in Frankfurt. The terrorist who last handled the bomb was not a passenger on the flight.*

and

> *The bomb was designed by Mu'Ay Al-Din ((Mughanniya)), a Lebanese national who lives in IR and who is supposedly Iran's expert on aircraft bombing and high-jacking operations. The bomb was constructed in LY and then shipped to GE for placement on the aircraft (NFI).*

CIA drug smuggling

Another popular theory was the one about a CIA drug smuggling project. This theory suggests that U.S. Central Intelligence Agency (CIA) agents had set up a protected drug route from Europe to the

United States—allegedly called *Operation Corea*—that allowed Syrian drug dealers, led by Monzer al-Kassar (who was involved with Oliver North in the Iran-Contra scandal) to ship heroin to the U.S. using Pan Am flights, in exchange for intelligence on Palestinian groups holding hostages in Syria. The CIA allegedly protected the suitcases containing the drugs and made sure they were not searched. On the day of the bombing, as the theory goes, terrorists exchanged suitcases: one with drugs for one with a bomb.

Time Magazine introduced another version of this theory, claiming that the American intelligence officers on PA 103 – Matthew Gannon and Maj. Charles McKee – had found out about the drug operation, and were headed to Washington to raise their concerns about its impact on their hostage rescue plans.

Juval Aviv introduced a variation of this story in October 1989. Aviv was the owner of Interfor Inc, a private investigation company based on Madison Avenue, New York. Aviv claimed to be a former Mossad officer who led the *Operation Wrath of God* team that assassinated members of *Black September* who were believed to have been responsible for the *Munich Massacre* in 1972. According to his theory, the CIA knew in advance that the baggage exchange would take place, but let it happen anyway, because the protected drugs route was a rogue operation, and the American intelligence officers on PA 103 – Matthew Gannon and Maj. Charles McKee – had found out about it, and were on their way to Washington to tell their superiors.

After PA 103, Aviv was employed by Pan Am as their lead investigator for the bombing. He submitted a report (the *Interfor* report) in October 1989, blaming the bombing on a CIA-protected drugs route (*Barrons* December 17, 1989). This scenario provided Pan Am with a credible defense against claims for compensation by relatives of victims, since, if the U.S. government had helped the bomb bypass Pan Am's security, the airline could hardly have been held liable. The Interfor report alleged *inter alia* that Khalid Jafaar, a Lebanese-American passenger with links to *Hezbollah*, had unwittingly brought the bomb on board thinking he was carrying drugs on behalf of Syrian drug dealers he supposedly worked for.

However, the New York court, which heard the civil case lodged by the U.S. relatives, rejected the Interfor allegations for lack of evidence. Aviv was never interviewed by either the Scottish police or the FBI in connection with PA 103. The theory of the CIA-protected suitcase was detailed as well in Patrick Pesnot's *Rendez-vous avec X* radio program on June 1998.[1]

In 1990 the protected suitcase theory was given a new lease of life by Lester Coleman in his book *Trail of the Octopus*. Coleman was a former journalist-turned-intelligence agent working with the *Drug Enforcement Administration* (DEA) while employed by *Defense Intelligence Agency* (DIA) in Cyprus. Coleman claimed to have seen Khalid Jafaar in the DEA office in Nicosia, Cyprus once again implying that Jafaar was a drugs mule, but this time for the DEA instead of Syrian drug dealers. In 1997, Coleman pleaded guilty to five counts of perjury in a Federal court after admitting that he submitted a false testimony in a civil litigation brought on behalf of the families of passengers killed in the bombing.

Coleman's theory gained impetus when British journalist Paul Foot wrote a glowing review of Coleman's book for the London Review of Books. But on March 31, 2004—four months before his death—Foot reverted to the orthodox Iran/PFLP-GC theory in an article he wrote for *The Guardian* entitled "Lockerbie's dirty secret".
The 1994 documentary film *The Maltese Double Cross – Lockerbie*, which included interviews with Lester Coleman and Juval Aviv, seemed to favour a hybrid version embracing both the CIA-protected suitcase and the drugs mule versions of the theory. Shortly after the film was broadcast by Channel 4 television on 11 May 1995, Aviv was indicted on fraud charges. Aviv was quick to claim that these were trumped-up charges, and in due course they were dropped. The film can be viewed on the internet by scrolling down to *Allan Francovich - The Maltese Double Cross*.

The Malta Connection

The fragment of clothes were traced to a Maltese merchant, *Tony*

Gauci, who became a key prosecution witness, testifying that he sold the clothes to a man of Libyan appearance. Gauci was interviewed 23 times giving contradictory evidence about who had bought the clothes, that person's age, appearance and the date of purchase but later identified *Abdelbaset Ali Mohmed Al Megrahi.* As Megrahi had only been in Malta on December that date was assumed to be the purchase date. However, an official report providing information not made available to the defense during the original trial stated that four days before identifying al-Megrahi for the first time, Gauci had seen a picture of al-Megrahi in a magazine which connected him to the bombing, a fact which could have distorted his judgment. The date is also in doubt as Gauci had testified that Malta's Christmas lights had not been on when the clothes had been purchased, it has since been found they had in fact been switched on 6 December. Scottish police had also failed to inform the defense that another witness had testified seeing Libyan men making a similar purchase on a different day.

Doubt has since been cast on the reliability of Gauci as a witness; five years after the trial, former Lord Advocate, Lord Fraser of Carmyllie, publicly described Gauci as being *"an apple short of a picnic"* and *"not quite the full shilling".* In addition, a legal source said that there was evidence that leading questions had been put to Gauci. In the BBC Two The Conspiracy Files: Lockerbie shown on August 31, 2008, it was claimed that one significant reason for Megrahi's latest appeal was that Gauci, who had picked him out in a line-up, had seen a magazine photograph of him just four days before he made the identification.

In October 2007, it was reported by the Guardian Newspaper that Gauci received a $2 million reward for testifying against Megrahi at the Lockerbie trial:

"The key prosecution witness in the Lockerbie bombing trial was allegedly offered a $2m reward in return for giving evidence, raising fresh doubts about the safety of the case.
Lawyers for Abdelbaset Ali Mohmed al-Megrahi, the Libyan convicted of

murdering 270 people on board Pan Am Flight 103, have evidence that detectives investigating the bombing recommended that Tony Gauci, a shopkeeper from Malta, be given the payment after the case ended.

Mr Gauci's testimony at the trial was crucial to al-Megrahi's conviction. He told the trial at Camp Zeist in the Netherlands that the Libyan had bought clothes at his shop which the prosecution claimed were packed into the suitcase bomb that exploded over Lockerbie on December 21 1988.

The defence team believe Mr Gauci may have received a larger sum from the US authorities. His role in the case is to be central to al-Megrahi's appeal against his conviction, which the Scottish Criminal Cases Review Commission said was unsafe.

They are to press for full disclosure of these payments, and the release of a potentially vital US document which is thought to cast doubt on official accounts about the timer allegedly used in the bombing, at an appeal hearing next week.

The secret document is believed to dispute prosecution claims that al-Megrahi used a digital timer bought from a Swiss company, Mebo, and then planted the bomb on a flight from Malta to Germany - a disclosure which would fatally undermine his conviction."

Timer fragment

A circuit board fragment, allegedly found embedded in a piece of charred material, was identified as part of an electronic timer similar to that found on a Libyan intelligence agent who had been arrested 10 months previously, carrying materials for a Semtex bomb. The timer allegedly was traced through its Swiss manufacturer, *Mebo*, to the Libyan military, and Mebo employee *Ulrich Lumpert* identified the fragment at al-Megrahi's trial. Mebo's owner, *Edwin Bollier*, later revealed that in 1991 he had declined an offer from the FBI of $4 million to testify that the timer fragment was part of a Mebo MST-13 timer supplied to Libya. On 18 July 2007, Ulrich Lumpert admitted he had lied at the trial. In a sworn affidavit before a Zurich notary public, Lumpert stated that he had stolen a prototype MST-13 timer printed circuit board from Mebo and gave it without permission on 22 June 1989, to *"an official person investigating the Lockerbie case"*. Dr Hans Köchler, UN observer at the Lockerbie trial, who was sent a copy of Lumpert's affidavit, said: *"The Scottish authorities are now obliged to investigate this situation. Not only has Mr Lumpert admitted to stealing a sample of the timer, but to the fact he gave it to an official and then lied in court"*

Among the mysteries surrounding this timer fragment is how, when, and by whom it was found. *"A lover and his lass"* found the fragment while strolling in the forest, according to one police source close to the case. A man found the fragment while walking his dog, according to another version. Or, in yet another story from a former investigator, police found it while combing the ground on their hands and knees. The latter became the accepted version when evidence was given at the trial. Testimony indicated that on January 13, 1989, three weeks after the bombing, two Scottish detectives engaged in a line search in woods near Lockerbie came upon a piece of charred material, later identified as the neckband of a grey Slalom-brand shirt. Because of the charring, it was sent for analysis to the DERA forensic explosives laboratory at Fort Halstead in Kent. It was not until May 12, 1989, that Dr Thomas Hayes examined the charred material. He teased out the cloth and found within it fragments of white paper, fragments of black plastic, a fragment of metal and a fragment of wire mesh—all subsequently found to be fragments of a Toshiba RT-SF 16 and its manual. Dr Hayes testified that he also found embedded a half-inch fragment of green circuit board.

The next reference to this circuit board fragment was on September 15, 1989, when Alan Feraday of DERA sent a Polaroid photograph of it to the police officer leading the investigation, Detective Chief Inspector William Williamson, asking for help in identification and with a covering note saying this was *"the best that I can do in such a short time."* In June 1990, Feraday and DCI Williamson were said to have visited FBI headquarters in Washington and together with Thomas Thurman, an FBI explosives expert, identified the fragment as coming from a type of timer circuit board similar to the one in the timer that had been seized from a Libyan intelligence agent, *Mohammad al-Marzouk,* who had been arrested in Dakar airport, Senegal ten months before PA 103 (*The Independent,* December 19, 1990). Marzouk was found to be carrying 9.5 pounds (4.3 kg) of

Semtex, several packets of TNT, 10 detonators, and an electronic timer—a so-called MST-13 timer—with the word Mebo printed on it. DERA's timer fragment, which was subsequently designated as PT/35(b), would eventually lead detectives via its Swiss manufacturer to Abdel Basset Ali al-Megrahi.

Thurman's involvement in identifying the fragment later proved controversial because of a 1997 report on the FBI laboratory, unrelated to the PA 103 investigation, written by U.S. Inspector-General Michael Bromwich, which concluded that Thurman had altered lab reports in ways that had rendered them inaccurate, and that he ought to be transferred to a position outside the FBI lab (*The Wall Street Journal*, September 26, 1997). Thurman was not called to testify. Potentially also damaging to the Crown's case as presented at the trial, the testimony of Thurman's UK counterpart, DERA's Alan Feraday, has now been called into question. In three separate cases—where Feraday had been the expert witness—men against whom he gave evidence have had their convictions overturned. And, thirdly, Dr Thomas Hayes was castigated for his failure to test the timer fragment for explosives residue, even though at the trial he maintained that the fragment was too small to test. Defence counsel contrasted Hayes' testimony with that of two of his colleagues at DERA's forensic laboratory (Elliott and Higgs) who, as revealed in the notorious *Maguire Seven* trial, had tested minute samples, from underneath the fingernails of the suspects, for explosives residue. In another important development, a retired senior Scottish police chief has added fuel to the timer fragment fire by claiming that the CIA planted this crucial piece of evidence.

The *Scottish Criminal Cases Review Commission* (SCCRC) has considered all of these issues and decided in June 2007 to refer Megrahi's case back for a fresh appeal. The second appeal will be heard by five judges at the *Court of Criminal Appeal*. A procedural hearing at the Appeal Court in Edinburgh took place on October 11, 2007 when prosecution and defence lawyers discussed legal issues with a panel of three judges. One of the issues concerns a number of documents from an undisclosed source country that were shown to the prosecution but were not disclosed to the defence. The documents are understood to relate to the Mebo MST-13 timer that allegedly detonated the PA103 bomb.

In January 2009, it was reported that, although Megrahi's second appeal against conviction is scheduled to begin on 27 April 2009, the hearing could last as long as 12 months because of the complexity of the case and volume of material to be examined.

Mebo

Investigators discovered that *Mebo* stood for *Meister & Bollier*, an electronics firm in Zürich, Switzerland. It emerged at the trial that one of the owners, Edwin Bollier, had sold 20 so-called MST-13 timers (identical to the one found in Senegal) to Libya in 1985, in the hope of winning a contract to supply the Libyan military. The first time he supplied a batch of timers he had accompanied Libyan officials to the desert city of *Sabha*, and had watched as his timers were used in explosions. He told the court that he had met Megrahi on that occasion for the first time, believing him to be a major in the Libyan army and a relative of Gaddafi's.

After that meeting, Bollier said that Megrahi and his co-accused, Fhimah, who he believed were good friends, had set up a travel business together under the name ABH in the Mebo offices in Zürich. Fhimah later went onto to become the station manager for Libyan Arab Airlines at Luqa Airport in Malta. (Fhimah has acknowledged he worked for the airline, but says he left the job three months before the bombing.)

Bollier testified at the trial that the Scottish police had originally shown him a fragment of a *brown 8-ply* circuit board, of a prototype timer which had never been supplied to Libya. Yet the sample he was asked to identify at the trial was a *green 9-ply* circuit board that Mebo had indeed supplied to Libya. Bollier wanted to pursue this discrepancy, but was told by trial Judge, Lord Sutherland, that he could not do so.

On July 18, 2007 Mebo's electronics engineer, Ulrich Lumpert, admitted he had given false evidence about the timer at the trial. In a sworn affidavit before a Zurich notary, Lumpert stated that he had stolen a prototype MST-13 timer PC-board from Mebo and gave it without permission on June 22, 1989, to *"an official person investigating the Lockerbie case"*. Dr Hans Köchler, UN observer at the Lockerbie trial, who was sent a copy of Lumpert's affidavit, said: *"The Scottish authorities are now obliged to investigate this situation. Not only has Mr Lumpert admitted to stealing a sample of the timer, but to the fact he gave it to an official and then lied in court"*.

In a documentary entitled *"Lockerbie revisited"* aired on 27 April 2009, the film's director and narrator, Gideon Levy, interviewed officials involved with the case. Former FBI laboratory scientist Fred Whitehurst described the FBI laboratory itself as a *"crime scene"*, where an unqualified colleague Thomas Thurman would routinely alter his scientific reports. The interviews also revealed that the timer fragment had never been tested for explosives residue due to "budgetary reasons". Thurman, who led the forensic investigation and identified the fragments' Libyan connection, confirmed that it was the *"only real piece of evidence against Libya"* and when asked of the importance of the timer in the conviction of al-Megrahi, FBI Task Force Chief Richard Marquise stated, *"It would be a very difficult case to prove ... I don't think we would ever (have) had an indictment"*.[

Unaccompanied suitcase

In parallel to the forensic work, detectives were also tracing the origin of every piece of luggage that had been checked onto PA 103, either in London or through the Interline baggage system. Interline baggage is baggage checked onto a flight in one location and automatically routed by the airline onto other locations. It is the weak link in airline security, because a bag not properly x-rayed by a low-risk airline in a low-risk airport may be routed without further checks through several other airports to high-risk airlines, so long as it is tagged correctly.

Frankfurt International Airport records for December 21, 1988, had been saved, only by chance, by computer programmer Bogomira Erac, who had kept a copy of the records on the spur of the moment *"... in memory of the people who were on the plane"*. These records were to show that an unaccompanied bag had been routed from Air Malta Flight KM 180 out of Luqa Airport to Frankfurt, where it had been loaded onto Pan Am 103A, the feeder flight to London. A properly marked Air Malta baggage tag would have routed the suitcase through the interline system from Malta to Frankfurt, Frankfurt to London, and London to New York.

The PA 103 investigators learned that the baggage for Air Malta Flight KM 180 was processed at the same time as the bags for Libyan Arab Airlines Flight 147 to Tripoli. They later discovered that Megrahi had been a passenger on this flight, having arrived in Malta two days earlier using a false passport. As he declined to take the stand during his trial, his explanation for his presence in Malta, and his reason for using a fake Identity card, was never heard.

Once alerted by Edwin Bollier of Mebo to the Megrahi–Fhimah friendship and business relationship, Scottish police obtained permission to search Fhimah's office in Malta. There they found a diary he had kept, in which he had reminded himself, on December 15, 1988, in English, to *"take taggs [sic] from Air Malta."*

However, Air Malta issued a statement in 1989, denying that an unaccompanied suitcase could have been carried on Flight KM 180: "39 passengers checked in 55 pieces of baggage; 55 pieces of baggage were loaded onto Flight KM 180; and, 39 passengers travelled on the flight. Air Malta has been informed that all 55 pieces of baggage have been accounted for and that every one of the 39 passengers has been identified," Air Malta declared.

Pan Am Flight 103 bombing trial

The **Pan Am Flight 103 bombing trial** began on 3 May 2000, 11 years, 4 months and 13 days after the blowing up of Pan Am Flight 103 on 21 December 1988. The 36-week trial took place at a specially convened *Scottish Court in the Netherlands* set up under Scots

Law and held at a disused United States Air Force base called Camp Zeist in Utrecht, in the Netherlands.

Upon the indictment of the two Libyan suspects in November 1991, the Libyan government was called upon to extradite them for trial in either the United Kingdom or the United States. Since no bilateral extradition treaty was in force between any of the three countries, Libya refused to hand the men over but did offer to detain them for trial in Libya, as long as all the incriminating evidence was provided. The offer was unacceptable to the US and UK, and there was an impasse for the next three years.

In November 1994, President Nelson Mandela offered South Africa as a neutral venue for the trial but this was rejected by the then British prime minister, John Major. A further three years elapsed until Mandela's offer was repeated to Major's successor, Tony Blair, when the president visited London in July 1997 and again at the 1997 Commonwealth Heads of Government Meeting (CHOGM) in Edinburgh in October 1997. At the latter meeting, Mandela warned that *"no one nation should be complainant, prosecutor and judge"* in the Lockerbie case.

The eventually agreed compromise solution of a trial in the Netherlands governed by Scots law was engineered by legal academic Professor Robert Black of Edinburgh University and, in accordance with the Labour government's promotion of an "ethical" foreign policy, was given political impetus by the then foreign secretary, Robin Cook. The Scottish Court in the Netherlands, a special High Court of Justiciary, was set up under Scots law in a disused United States Air Force base called Camp Zeist in Utrecht, in the Netherlands. A Scottish High Court of Justiciary was purpose-built at the neutral venue of Camp Zeist, Netherlands, a former United States Air Force base. Facilities for a high security prison were also installed there. Under a bilateral treaty between the United Kingdom and the Netherlands, these premises were, for the duration of the trial and any subsequent appeal, under the authority and control of the Scottish Court. Dutch law still theoretically applied to the area, but, barring an emergency, the Dutch authorities were banned from entering the premises and the Court had the authority to enact regulations that superseded Dutch law when necessary for the execution of the trial, and to jail people for contempt of court. The court itself, as well as people involved in the trial also enjoyed total or partial immunity from Dutch law.

Accused

Two Libyans, *Abdelbaset Ali Mohmed Al Megrahi* and *Al Amin Khalifa Fhimah*, were accused of the crime. In the run-up to the trial, the prosecution considered bringing charges against Swiss businessman, *Edwin Bollier*, of the electronics firm Mebo AG, but decided that, unless evidence to incriminate Bollier were to be introduced during the trial, he would not be included as a co-conspirator in causing the bombing.

Libya made three stipulations, when agreeing to hand over the two accused to the Scottish police: that they would not be interviewed by the police; no one else in Libya would be sought for the bombing; and, that the trial should be before three Scottish judges, sitting without a jury. On 5 April 1999, over a year ahead of the start of the trial, Megrahi and Fhimah arrived in the Netherlands.

Charges

The two accused denied all charges against them. Three outline charges were:

- murder;

- conspiracy to murder; and,

- a breach of the *Aviation Security Act 1982*.

The full charges included the names of the murdered 259 passengers and crew of Pan Am Flight 103, and the eleven residents killed at

Lockerbie in Scotland.

Judges

The Scottish High Court of Justiciary at Camp Zeist, Netherlands was presided over by three senior judges and an additional judge (non-voting).

Case

The case against the two defendants rested primarily on three points:

1. *that the bomb timer used was from a batch sold by a Swiss firm, Mebo AG to Libya;*

2. *a former colleague in the Libyan Airlines office in Malta, Abdulmajid Gialka, who was due to testify that he had seen the construction of the bomb, or at least its loading onto the plane at Frankfurt;*

3. *that the clothes identified as having been in the bomb suitcase had been bought by the defendant Megrahi at a shop in Malta.*

Each of these points was contested by the defence.

Edwin Bollier, the co-founder of the Swiss manufacturer of the timer, testified that he had sold similar timers to East Germany, and admitted having connections to a number of intelligence agencies, including both the Libyans and the CIA.

Gialka, by the time of the trial was living under the *Witness Protection Program* in the US, had connections with the CIA prior to 1988, and stood to collect up to $4m in reward money following a conviction.

Tony Gauci, the Maltese shopkeeper, failed to positively identify Megrahi in nineteen separate pre-trial statements to the police. In court, Gauci was asked five times if he recognised anyone in the courtroom, without replying. Only when the prosecutor pointed to Megrahi did Gauci say that "he resembles him". On a previous occasion Gauci had identified *Abu Talb* (who the defence contended was the real bomber) saying that Talb resembled the customer "a lot". Gauci's police statements identified the customer as over 6 feet tall and over 50 years of age; Megrahi is 5 feet 8 inches, and in late 1988 was 36.

The clothes purchase took place on either 23 November or 7 December 1988; Megrahi was only in Malta on 7 December. Gauci recalled the customer also buying an umbrella due to the rain. The defence argued, using meteorological records, that it rained all day on 23 November, but only briefly or not at all on 7 December.

In its closing arguments, the prosecution stressed that Megrahi could not have planted the bomb without the assistance of Fhimah - both defendants were equally guilty, and should stand or fall together.

Proceedings (May 2000 - Jan 2001)

Court proceedings started on 3 May 2000 with the prosecution outlining the case against the accused and previewing the evidence which they expected would satisfy the judges *beyond reasonable doubt* that the sabotage of PA 103 was caused by:

- the explosion of an *improvised explosive device* (IED);

- an IED that was contained within a Toshiba radio cassette player in a hard-shell Samsonite suitcase along with various items of clothing which had been bought in Mary's House, Sliema, Malta;

- an IED triggered by the use of an MST-13 timer, manufactured by Mebo Ag in Switzerland; and,

- the so-called *primary suitcase* being introduced as

unaccompanied baggage at Luqa Airport in Malta, conveyed by Air Malta flight KM180 to Frankfurt International Airport, transferred there onto feeder flight PA 103A to Heathrow Airport, loaded into the interline baggage container AVE 4041PA at Heathrow, and put on board PA 103 in the forward cargo hold.

In the trial's second week, Detective Constable Gilchrist was asked about the piece of charred material that he and DC McColm had found three weeks after the PA 103 crash. DC Gilchrist attached a label to the material and wrote "Cloth (charred)" on it. The word 'cloth' was overwritten by the word 'debris'. DC Gilchrist's attempts to explain the overwriting were later described by the judges as "at worst evasive and at best confusing."

There was no third week and, because of equipment problems in the courtroom, only a truncated fourth week.

In week 5, Professor Peel of the Defence Evaluation and Research Agency (DERA) gave evidence concerning the baggage container AVE 4041PA.

Week 6 was devoted to the testimony behind screens of CIA agents and Bureau of Alcohol, Tobacco and Firearms officers relating to interception of arms caches (including MST-13 timers) in the West African countries of Senegal and Togo.

In week 7 Alan Feraday, also of DERA, gave evidence. Feraday presented the court with a simulated IED of the type alleged to have caused the sabotage of PA 103. Under cross-examination, he admitted the fragments of radio cassette and timer, found in DC Gilchrist's *cloth/debris (charred)* material, had not been tested for explosives residue. The defence were, however, later criticized for having failed to challenge Feraday to explain why his note to Detective Chief Inspector William Williamson in September 1989, covering a Polaroid photograph of the timer fragment (identified in May 1989), said it was "the best I can do in such a short time."

Later in week 7, the co-founder of Mebo AG, Erwin Meister, testified that Mebo had supplied Libya with 20 MST-13 timing devices, and identified one of the two accused (Megrahi) as a former business contact. The defence asked Meister, under cross-examination, to explain the purpose of his visit to Syria in 1984.

Meister's partner, Edwin Bollier, was questioned in week 8. Bollier said Mebo made a range of products including briefcases equipped to radio-detonate IEDs. He agreed that Mebo had sold 20 MST-13 timers to Libya in 1985 which were later tested by Libyan special forces at their base at Sabha. Bollier said: *"I was present when two such timers were included in bomb cylinders"*. In court, Bollier was shown a number of printed circuit board fragments which he identified as coming from the Mebo MST-13 timer, but he claimed that these timer fragments appeared to have been modified.

Joachim Wenzel, an employee of the Stasi, the former East German intelligence agency, testified behind screens in week 9. Wenzel claimed to have been Bollier's handler in the years 1982-85 and testified that Mebo had supplied the Stasi with timers.
Former Mebo employee, Ulrich Lumpert, confirmed that as an electronics engineer he had produced all of the firm's MST-13 timers. Lumpert agreed that the fragments shown to him in court "could be" from that timer and was asked to confirm his signature on a letter concerning a technical fault with the prototype MST-13 timer. The trial was then adjourned until 12 July 2000.

Note:

On 18 July 2007 Lumpert admitted he had lied at the trial. In a sworn affidavit before a Zurich notary, Lumpert stated that he had stolen a prototype MST-13 timer PC-board from Mebo and gave it without permission on 22 June 1989, to "an official person investigating the Lockerbie case".

See also the Observer 2 September 2007:

Vital Lockerbie evidence 'was tampered with'

Fragments of bomb timer that helped to convict a Libyan ex-agent were 'practically carbonised' before the trial, says bankrupt Swiss businessman

The Observer, *Sunday 2 September 2007*

Article history

The key piece of material evidence used by prosecutors to implicate Libya in the Lockerbie bombing has emerged as a probable fake.

Nearly two decades after Pan Am flight 103 exploded over Scotland on 21 December, 1988, allegations of international political intrigue and shoddy investigative work are being levelled at the British government, the FBI and the Scottish police as one of the crucial witnesses, Swiss engineer Ulrich Lumpert, has apparently confessed that he lied about the origins of a crucial 'timer' - evidence that helped tie the man convicted of the bombing to the crime.

The disaster killed 270 people when the London to New York Boeing 747 exploded in mid-air. Britain and the US blamed Libya, saying that its leader, Colonel Muammar Gadaffi, wanted revenge for the US bombing of Tripoli in 1986. At a trial in the Netherlands in 2001, former Libyan agent Abdulbaset al-Megrahi was jailed for life.

He is currently serving his sentence in Greenock prison, but later this month the Scottish Court of Appeal is expected to hear Megrahi's case, after the Scottish Criminal Cases Review Commission ruled in June that there was enough evidence to suggest a miscarriage of justice. Lumpert's confession, which was given to police in his home city of Zurich last week, will strengthen Megrahi's appeal.
The Zurich-based Swiss businessman Edwin Bollier, who has spent nearly two decades trying to clear his company's name, is as eager for the appeal as is Megrahi. Bollier's now bankrupt company, Mebo, manufactured the timer switch that prosecutors used to implicate Libya after they said that fragments of it had been found on a Scottish hillside.

Bollier, now 70, admits having done business with Libya. 'Two years before Lockerbie, we sold 20 MST-13 timers to the Libyan military. FBI agents and the Scottish investigators said one of those timers had been used to detonate the bomb. We were shown a fuzzy photograph and I confirmed the fragments looked as though they came from one of our timers.'

However, Bollier was uneasy with the photograph he had been shown and asked to see the fragments. He was finally given permission in 1998 and travelled to Dumfries to see the evidence.

'I was shown fragments of a brown circuit board which matched our prototype. But when the MST-13 went into production, the timers contained green boards. I knew that the timers sold to Libya had green boards. I told the investigators this.'

Back in Switzerland, Bollier's company was in effect bankrupt, having faced a lawsuit from Pan Am and having lost major clients, such as the German federal police to which Mebo supplied communications equipment.

In 2001, Bollier spent five days in the witness box at the Lockerbie trial at Camp Zeist in the Netherlands. 'I was a defence witness, but the trial was so skewed to prove Libyan involvement that the details of what I had to say was ignored. A photograph of the fragments was produced in court and I asked to see the pieces again. When they were brought to me, they were practically carbonised. They had been tampered with since I had seen them in Dumfries.'

Few people apart from conspiracy theorists and investigative journalists working on the case were prepared to believe Bollier until the end of last month, when Lumpert, one of his former employees, walked into a Zurich police station and asked to swear an affidavit before a notary.

Dr Hans Köchler, UN observer at the Lockerbie trial, who was sent a copy of Lumpert's affidavit, said: *"The Scottish authorities are now obliged to investigate this situation. Not only has Mr Lumpert admitted to stealing a sample of the timer, but to the fact he gave it to an official and then lied in court"*.

In week 11, Mebo lawyer Dieter Neupert filed an official criminal complaint against the Crown over what he alleged was a *'forged fragment of MST-13 timer'*. Tony Gauci of Mary's House, Sliema in Malta, testified that he had sold a number of items of clothing to one of the defendants, Megrahi. Wilfred Borg, Ground Operations Manager at Malta's Luqa airport, was questioned about Luqa's baggage handling procedures. A Mr Ferrugia confirmed that he had been a passenger on Air Malta flight KM 180 to Frankfurt on 21 December 1988.

Two Germans, Birgit Seliger and Evelin Steinwandt, confirmed in week 12 that they had also travelled on flight KM 180. Martin Huebner and Joachim Koscha were questioned about baggage handling procedures at Frankfurt airport.

Five more passengers on flight KM 180 testified in week 13. The captain of flight KM 180, Khalil Lahoud, also gave evidence and was asked to confirm that the aircraft's altitude during the flight had exceeded 30,000 ft. This information was intended to demonstrate that an IED loaded at Luqa airport would have had a timed detonator rather than a barometric trigger. The trial was then adjourned until 22 August 2000.

In week 17, another four passengers on flight KM 180 were asked to testify. The following week, Abdul Majid Giaka, a defector from the Libyan intelligence service, appeared wearing sunglasses and a wig. Giaka, who had been on the US Witness Protection Program since July 1991, testified that Megrahi was a Libyan agent.

Rather than calling the defendants to the witness stand, their legal team sought to use the special defence of incrimination against the person or persons they believed were guilty of the crime. There was speculation that *Mohammed Abu Talb*, a convicted PFLP-GC member, would be called by the defence to testify in week 19, and when he failed to appear the trial was adjourned for the next five weeks to allow new evidence from a "country in the Mid East" to be examined.

One of the last witnesses for the prosecution was broadcaster and politician, Pierre Salinger, who was questioned by prosecutor Alan Turnbull and by both defence counsel William Taylor and Richard Keen.

But Pierre Salinger, former chief foreign correspondent for the ABC network, was infuriated when the court would not allow him to name who he believed was to blame. Mr Salinger said:

"I know that these two Libyans had nothing to do with it. I know who did it and I know exactly why it was done."

He was based at ABC's London office when the two accused were indicted in 1991. The court heard that Mr Salinger, who appeared as a prosecution witness, had interviewed the two standing trial.
Judges were shown extracts from the interview in which Mr Megrahi strongly denied being involved. He added he had never been a member of the Libyan intelligence agency, and his family and countrymen would be "ashamed" to do such a job. Mr Megrahi said he had not been in Malta on the day the bomb began its journey to Heathrow via Frankfurt.

Mr Salinger was then asked about how he had obtained the meeting, but he was stopped from giving his views on the case. After Alan Turnbull QC, prosecuting, and defence counsel William Taylor QC and Richard Keen QC finished their questioning, the trial judge, Lord Sutherland, asked Mr Salinger to leave the witness box. The broadcaster said:

"That's all? You're not letting me tell the truth. Wait a minute, I know exactly who did it. I know how it was done."

Lord Sutherland interrupted and told the witness:

"If you wish to make a point you may do so elsewhere, but I'm afraid you may not do so in this court."

The defence also called Abu Talb to the witnessstand. Abu Talb was born in Port Said in Egypt. He was a soldier in the Egyptian Army and also received training in the Soviet Union. He joined the Palestine Liberation Organization (PLO) in 1970. He has asserted that he deserted from the Egyptian Army in the mid-1970s and thereafter fled to Lebanon via Jordan with a false passport. He joined the Palestinian Popular Struggle Front (PPSF) in 1974 and participated on its side during the early stages of the Lebanese Civil War. There, he rose to the rank of lieutenant, commanding a 100-member security detail. He also went to Beirut, where he was wounded in fighting in 1976 and spent the next two years studying politics and economics at the University of Beirut.

In 1986, Talb arrived in Sweden from Syria with his wife and child on a false Moroccan passport, under the name of Belaid Massoud Ben Hadi, and was granted political asylum there. He settled in Uppsala and ran a store specializing in Arab foods and videotapes.

In May 1989, Talb was arrested in connection with the bombing of Pan Am Flight 103 on 21 December 1988, where 270 people were killed. He came under suspicion after Swedish investigators established that he had travelled to Malta in October 1988, two months before the bombing. The Scottish investigators earlier found that the bomb was hidden in a radio-cassette recorder, which was placed in a suitcase and wrapped in clothing bought in Malta. In Talb's apartment in Uppsala, the police also found a 1988 calendar with the date "21 December" circled. In addition, Talb's wife was recorded in a wiretapped telephone call warning another unidentified Palestinian to "get rid of the clothes immediately." Talb denied he was involved in the bombing and said his trip to Malta was for "business".

In a special defence at the Pan Am Flight 103 bombing trial, defence counsel alleged that the Syrian-backed Popular Front for the Liberation of Palestine-General Command (PFLP-GC) and the lesser known PPSF were responsible for blowing up Pan Am Flight 103. They called Abu Talb to give evidence at the trial since they alleged he was linked to both terrorist groups. Instead, Abu Talb appeared as a prosecution witness, and in his testimony in November 2000, he told the court that he was not involved in the December 1988 Lockerbie bombing. He said he had been at home babysitting in Sweden at the time of the bombing.

The Crown concluded the prosecution case in week 26. In its closing address for Fhimah in weeks 26 and 27, the defence submitted there was no case for him to answer. There were no weeks 28 to 32.

The expected documents from the *"country in the Mid East"* - thought to be Syria - had not materialized by week 33, and the defence confirmed that the accused would not take the witness stand. The prosecution dropped two of the three charges against the accused, leaving the single charge of murder against both Megrahi and Fhimah. The defence claimed the accused had no case to answer.

In week 34 the defence argued that the IED started its journey at Heathrow, rather than Luqa airport in Malta. The judges then retired to consider their verdict.

There was no week 35. The judges announced their verdict on 31 January 2001 in week 36.

Verdicts (Jan 2001)

In addition to the options of guilty and not guilty, a third verdict of not proven was available to the judges under Scots Law. The judges announced their verdicts on 31 January 2001. The judgement stated:

"From the evidence which we have discussed so far, we are satisfied that it has been proved that the primary suitcase containing the explosive device was dispatched from Malta, passed through Frankfurt and was loaded onto PA103 at Heathrow. It is, as we have said, clear that with one exception the clothing in the primary suitcase was the clothing purchased in Mr Gauci's shop on 7 December 1988. The purchaser was, on Mr Gauci's evidence, a Libyan. The trigger for the explosion was an MST-13 timer of the single solder mask

variety. A substantial quantity of such timers had been supplied to Libya. We cannot say that it is impossible that the clothing might have been taken from Malta, united somewhere with a timer from some source other than Libya and introduced into the airline baggage system at Frankfurt or Heathrow. When, however, the evidence regarding the clothing, the purchaser and the timer is taken with the evidence that an unaccompanied bag was taken from KM180 to PA103A, the inference that that was the primary suitcase becomes, in our view, irresistible. As we have also said, the absence of an explanation as to how the suitcase was taken into the system at Luqa is a major difficulty for the Crown case but after taking full account of that difficulty, we remain of the view that the primary suitcase began its journey at Luqa. The clear inference which we draw from this evidence is that the conception, planning and execution of the plot which led to the planting of the explosive device was of Libyan origin. While no doubt organisations such as the PFLP-GC and the PPSF were also engaged in terrorist activities during the same period, we are satisfied that there was no evidence from which we could infer that they were involved in this particular act of terrorism, and the evidence relating to their activities does not create a reasonable doubt in our minds about the Libyan origin of this crime."

The judges were unanimous in finding the second accused, Al Amin Khalifa Fhimah, not guilty of the murder charge. Fhimah was freed and he returned to his home at Souk al-Juma in Libya on 1 February 2001. As for Abdelbaset Ali Mohmed Al Megrahi the judges said:

"There is nothing in the evidence which leaves us with any reasonable doubt as to the guilt of the first accused, and accordingly we find him guilty of the remaining charge in the indictment as amended."

Megrahi was sentenced to life imprisonment, with a recommendation that he should serve at least 20 years before being eligible for parole.

Appeal (Jan 2001 - March 2002)

The defence team had 14 days in which to appeal against Megrahi's conviction on 31 January 2001, and a further six weeks to submit the full grounds of the appeal. These were considered by a judge sitting in private who decided to grant Megrahi leave to appeal. The only basis for an appeal under Scots law is that there has been a *"miscarriage of justice"* which is not defined in statute and so it is for the appeal court to determine the meaning of these words in each case. Because three judges and one alternate judge had presided over the trial, five judges were required to preside over the *Court of Criminal Appeal:*

- Lord Cullen, Lord Justice-General
- Lord Kirkwood
- Lord Osborne
- Lord Macfadyen, *and*
- Lord Nimmo Smith

In what was described as a milestone in Scottish legal history, Lord Cullen granted the BBC permission in January 2002 to televise the appeal, and to broadcast it on the *Internet* in English with a simultaneous Arabic translation.

William Taylor QC, leading the defence, said at the appeal's opening on 23 January 2002 that the three trial judges sitting without a jury had failed to see the relevance of *"significant"* evidence and had accepted unreliable facts. He argued that the verdict was not one that a reasonable jury in an ordinary trial could have reached if it were given proper directions by the judge. The grounds of the appeal rested on two areas of evidence where the defence claimed the original court was mistaken:

- *A1. The court erred in finding that the date of the purchase of the clothes from the shop at Mary's House, 63 Tower Street, Sliema, Malta, was December 7 1988. There was no proper basis on the evidence for the finding that the date of the purchase of the clothes was either November 23 or December 7 1988.*

- *A4. The court failed to advance adequate reasons for preferring Gauci's identification of the appellant by resemblance of a photo, at identification parade and in court, to earlier descriptions of the purchaser which did not match the appellant.*

- *A5. The court failed to deal with and resolve the contradictions and inconsistencies in the evidence of Gauci regarding the date of the purchase and the identity of the purchaser.*

- *A6. The evidence of identification was not of such character, quality or strength to justify a finding that the appellant was the clothes buyer. The court failed properly to take account of the significant body of evidence referred to above which pointed away from December 7 as the date of purchase.*

- *B1. The court misdirected itself as to the accuracy of the records from Frankfurt Airport from which it found that an inference could be drawn that an unaccompanied bag travelled on KM 180 from Luqa airport to Frankfurt and was there loaded on to PA103A.*

- *B4. The documents and other evidence from Frankfurt, properly construed, were not of sufficient strength, quality or character to enable the court to conclude that an unaccompanied bag from KM 180 was transferred to and loaded on to PA103A.*

- *B10. The court failed to take account of the defence submission that the fact that the primary suitcase was located at or near to the optimum position to achieve its destructive purpose gave rise to an inference that the device was ingested at Heathrow airport.*

- *B11. There exists significant evidence which was not heard at the trial. It demonstrates that at some time in the two hours before 12.35am on December 21 1988 a padlock had been forced on a secure door giving access to airside in Terminal 3 of Heathrow Airport, near to the area referred to in the trial as the "baggage build-up area".*

Had this evidence been available at the trial it would have supported the body of evidence suggestive of the bomb having been infiltrated at Heathrow.

On 14 March 2002 it took Lord Cullen less than three minutes to deliver the decision of the High Court of Justiciary. The five judges rejected the appeal, ruling unanimously that

"none of the grounds of appeal was well-founded",

adding

"this brings proceedings to an end".

The following day, a helicopter took Megrahi from Camp Zeist to continue his life sentence in Barlinnie Prison, Glasgow.

Remarks by Lord Fraser

The Sunday Times of 23 October 2005 reported that Lord Fraser of Carmyllie, who drew up the 1991 indictment against the two accused Libyans and issued warrants for their arrest, had now cast doubt upon the reliability of the main prosecution witness, Tony Gauci. Lord Fraser criticised the Maltese shopkeeper for *inter alia* being "not quite the full shilling" and an "apple short of a picnic".

The then Lord Advocate, Lord Boyd, reacted to the remarks, as follows:

"It was Lord Fraser who, as Lord Advocate, initiated the Lockerbie prosecution. At no stage, then or since, has he conveyed any reservation about any aspect of the prosecution to those who worked on the case, or to anyone in the prosecution service."

Lord Boyd has asked Lord Fraser to clarify his apparent attack on Gauci by issuing a public statement of explanation.

William Taylor QC, who defended Megrahi at the trial and the appeal, said Lord Fraser should never have presented Gauci as a crown witness:

> *"A man who has a public office, who is prosecuting in the criminal courts in Scotland, has got a duty to put forward evidence based upon*

people he considers to be reliable. He was prepared to advance Gauci as a witness of truth in terms of identification and, if he had these misgivings about him, they should have surfaced at the time. The fact that he is coming out many years later after my former client has been in prison for nearly four and a half years is nothing short of disgraceful. Gauci's evidence was absolutely central to the conviction and for Peter Fraser not to realise that is scandalous," Taylor said.

Tam Dalyell, former Labour MP who played a crucial role in organising the trial at Camp Zeist in the Netherlands, described Lord Fraser's remarks as an 'extraordinary development':

"I think there is an obligation for the chairman and members of the Scottish Criminal Cases Review Commission to ask Lord Fraser to see them and testify under oath - it's that serious. Fraser should have said this at the time and, if not then, he was under a moral obligation to do so before the trial at Zeist. I think there will be all sorts of consequences," Dalyell declared.

Gerard Sinclair, chief executive of the SCCRC, refused to say whether the Commission was investigating Lord Fraser's reported remarks. *"Any investigation we carry out we seek to do so as rigorously and as thoroughly as possible,"* he said.

Robert Black, Professor Emeritus of Scots Law at Edinburgh University and a Lockerbie expert, described the alleged remarks as *"an indication that various people who have been involved in the Lockerbie prosecution are now positioning themselves in anticipation of the SCCRC holding that there was a prima facie miscarriage of justice, and sending it back for a fresh appeal."*

UN observer

Professor Hans Köchler, who was appointed as one of the UN observers by UN Secretary-General Kofi Annan, criticised the trial in his report and evaluation. Köchler observed that the trial had been politically influenced in breach of legal traditions and principles, such as the Rule of law. In an interview for the BBC on the day the first appeal was rejected, he described the court's decision as a *"spectacular miscarriage of justice"*.

In a radio programme entitled Politics and justice: the *Lockerbie trial*, which was broadcast on 9 September 2007 by Australia's ABC Radio National, Dr Köchler, Robert Black and Jim Swire expressed their views on the Lockerbie trial and the first appeal, and suggested what should happen next.

In the June 2008 edition of the Scottish lawyers' magazine The Firm, Köchler referred to the *'totalitarian'* nature of the ongoing second Lockerbie appeal process saying it "bears the hallmarks of an *'intelligence operation'*."

SCCRC review (Sep 2003 - June 2007)

The *Scottish Criminal Cases Review Commission* (SCCRC), which was established by Act of Parliament in April 1999, has wide-ranging powers to investigate cases where a miscarriage of justice is alleged, and reviewed Megrahi's case from September 2003. Although the Commission normally expects to review a case and announce its decision within 12 months, it took nearly four years to complete the Megrahi review. On 28 June 2007 the SCCRC published a summary of its 800-page report and referred Megrahi's conviction to the *Court of Criminal Appeal* for a fresh appeal:

NEWS RELEASE
ABDELBASET ALI MOHMED AL MEGRAHI

28 June 2007

The Scottish Criminal Cases Review Commission ("the Commission") has today referred the case of Abdelbaset Ali Mohmed Al Megrahi ("the applicant") to the High Court of Justiciary.

As a result of the Commission's decision the applicant is entitled to a further appeal against his conviction for the murder of 270 people who died following the bombing of Pam Am flight 103 over Lockerbie, Scotland on 21 December 1988.

In accordance with the Commission's statutory obligations, a statement of the reasons for its decision has been sent to the High Court, the applicant, his solicitor, and Crown Office. The Commission has no power under statute to make copies of its statements of reasons available to the public. However, given the worldwide interest in this case, and the fact that there has been a great deal of press and media speculation as to the nature of the grounds of review, the Commission has decided to provide a fuller news release than normal. Accordingly, a brief summary of some of the Commission's main findings in the case is given below.

As the full statement of reasons extends to over 800 pages and is accompanied by a further thirteen volumes of appendices it is not possible to reflect the detail or complexity of the issues that have been addressed by the Commission. This news release is intended therefore merely to assist in an understanding of the nature of the Commission's main investigations and findings and does not form part of its decision in the case.

Announcing the decision today, the Chairman of the Commission the Very Rev. Dr Graham Forbes CBE said: - *"The Commission has a very special role within the Scottish Criminal Justice system, and has been given extensive statutory powers to enable it to carry out this role. The function of the Commission is not to decide upon the guilt or innocence of an applicant. We are neither pro-Crown nor pro-defence. Our role is to examine the grounds of review identified, either by the applicant, a third party or by our own investigations, and to decide whether any of the grounds meet our statutory test. I am satisfied that the Commission has vigorously and independently scrutinised the many grounds of review in this particular application, and has now produced a lengthy and detailed statement of reasons which I believe comprehensively deals with all of the issues raised."*

Provost Forbes continued:- *"It would have been impossible for us to have completed our investigation without the cooperation of other public and government bodies both at home and abroad, and we readily acknowledge this help. I would emphasise however that neither Scottish Ministers nor the Scottish Executive Justice Department, nor for that matter any other official body, has at any time sought to influence or interfere in the Commission's investigations; and all requests for appropriate grant aid to enable a full and comprehensive investigation and review have been properly met, without question.*

This has been a difficult case to deal with. The Commission's enquiry team have worked tirelessly for over three years. Some of what we have discovered may imply innocence; some of what we have discovered may imply guilt. However, such matters are for a court to decide. The Commission is of the view, based upon our lengthy investigations, the new evidence we have found and other evidence which was not before the trial court that the applicant may have suffered a miscarriage of justice. The place for that matter to be determined is in the appeal court, to which we now refer the case."

Gerard Sinclair, the Chief Executive of the Commission said today: - *"This has clearly been a unique case for the Commission in many ways, not least, in terms of the universal press and media interest. It has certainly been the longest, the most expensive and singularly most complex case we have had to investigate and review. I am pleased that after a full and thorough investigation we are now able to produce our statement of reasons. It has been difficult at times to ignore, and to refrain from commenting upon, the almost constant speculation regarding this review, much of which I have to say has been either inaccurate or simply incorrect. I hope however that the comprehensive statement of reasons which the Commission has now produced for the parties will answer the many questions which have been raised over the last 3 years. The Commission's involvement in the case is now at an end. It is a matter entirely for those representing the Crown and the defence at any future appeal to decide whether they wish to rely upon the conclusions reached by the Commission, or develop arguments of their own. Thereafter, it will be for the appeal court to decide whether there has been a miscarriage of justice in this case."*

1. 0 Background

1.1 On 31 January 2001, following a trial at the High Court of Justiciary sitting in the Netherlands ("the trial court"), the applicant, a Libyan national, was convicted by three Scottish judges of murdering those who died as a result of the bombing of PA103. A co-accused, Al Amin Khalifa Fhimah, also a Libyan, was found not guilty. The applicant's appeal against conviction was rejected by the High Court on 14 March 2002. Although appeals by both the Crown and the applicant in relation to the sentence are still ongoing, those proceedings are entirely separate from the Commission's role in the case which concerned only the conviction.

2.0 The Review

2.1 The applicant applied to the Commission for a review of his conviction on 23 September 2003. The application, which comprised 16 separate volumes of submissions and supporting materials, contained numerous grounds on which it was argued the case should be referred to the High Court. In February 2004 the Commission allocated the case to an investigative team consisting of a senior legal officer (Robin Johnston) and two legal officers (Andrew Beadsworth and Gordon Newall). An additional legal officer (Michael Walker) was involved in the case on a part time basis.

2.2 Throughout 2004 the firm of solicitors representing the applicant at that time lodged with the Commission a further five sets of submissions, the contents of which significantly broadened the scope of the initial application. The Commission also received and considered numerous submissions from other parties.

2.3 Correspondence was also received from the relatives of some of the victims who enquired mainly as to progress in the investigation.

2.4 During its investigation of the case the Commission had access to a wide range of materials including the following:

- the transcript of the evidence and submissions at trial;
- the Crown and defence productions at trial;
- all witness statements obtained by the police during its investigation including an electronic database of over 15,000 such statements;
- copies of all witness statements obtained by the Crown in preparation for the trial;
- the correspondence files prepared by the firm of solicitors which acted for the applicant at trial and in his appeal against conviction, and copies of all witness statements obtained by them from witnesses based in the United Kingdom;
- an electronic database consisting of all information held on the case by the firm of solicitors which acted for co-accused at trial.

2.5 As the custodians of much of the evidence in the case, Dumfries & Galloway Police were the Commission's principal source of additional information, receiving over 200 separate written requests for information from the Commission. In addition numerous visits were made to Dumfries police office where members of the enquiry team were given access to material held there. The Commission's enquiry team was also given access to materials held by the Forensic Explosives Laboratory at Fort Halstead, Kent, which dealt with the forensic examination of items during the police investigation. A substantial amount of information was also obtained from other agencies including Crown Office and the

Security Service.

2.6 The Commission's further enquiries were wide-ranging and took place in the United Kingdom, Malta, Libya and Italy from 2004 onwards. As well as examining the information provided to it, the Commission interviewed a further 45 witnesses, including the applicant and his co accused Mr Fhimah. Many of these interviews were conducted over several days and a number of the witnesses required to be seen on more than one occasion. Enquiries in Malta and Italy also involved the recovery of official records from various bodies.

2.7 As the Commission's statutory powers do not extend beyond Scotland, some difficulties were encountered where witnesses living in other countries refused to be interviewed. In the majority of cases these difficulties were resolved through discussions with the individuals concerned, but in respect of several witnesses living in Malta this was not possible. Accordingly at an early stage of the review an approach was made to the Attorney General of Malta to establish whether the Commission could make use of the provisions of Maltese law to obtain statements from the witnesses concerned. The Commission was advised by the Attorney General that in order to do so a written agreement between the United Kingdom and Malta would be required. Following a meeting with the Foreign and Commonwealth Office ("FCO"), in July 2005 the Commission drafted and sent such an agreement to the FCO which thereafter forwarded it to the Maltese authorities. After lengthy negotiations the agreement was signed by the United Kingdom and Maltese authorities in June 2006. The witnesses in question were interviewed by the Commission's enquiry team in August of that year.

2.8 The Commission continued to interview witnesses and examine productions during 2006 and 2007, and concluded its investigations in April 2007. Between the initial submissions and the additional submissions received during the course of the review, the Commission identified a total of 48 principal grounds for consideration and review by the Commission. In addition, as a result of our own investigations the Commission identified some further potential grounds of review. Many of the original grounds were the subject of numerous separate submissions and allegations submitted over many hundreds of pages. In relation to 45 of the original 48 grounds identified, the Commission has concluded that it does not believe that a miscarriage of justice has occurred. Of the remaining grounds, some of which resulted from the Commission's own investigations, the Commission has identified 6 grounds where it believes that a miscarriage of justice may have occurred and that it is in the interests of justice to refer the matter to the court of appeal.

3.0 The evidence at trial

3.1 In order to understand the Commission's findings in the case it is helpful to summarise the evidence on which the applicant's conviction is based.

3.2 The trial court found that the bomb which destroyed PA103 was contained within a Toshiba RT-SF16 radio cassette player which had been placed inside a brown hardshell Samsonite suitcase (known as "the primary suitcase"). Also established to have been inside the primary suitcase were twelve items of clothing and an umbrella, a number of which were traced to a shop called Mary's House in Sliema, Malta. When interviewed by the police, the proprietor of Mary's House, Anthony Gauci, recalled selling many of the items to a man he described as Libyan.

3.3 It was established that the bomb had been triggered by a digital timer known as an MST-13 which was manufactured by a firm based in Switzerland named MEBO. The trial court accepted the evidence given by one of the partners in that firm, Edwin Bollier, that in 1985 and 1986 he had supplied 20 sample MST-13 timers to Libya.

3.4 The trial court also found that the primary suitcase had been placed on board Air Malta flight KM180 from Malta to Frankfurt where it was transferred via the baggage system to Pam Am flight 103A ("PA103A") from Frankfurt to Heathrow, and thereafter to PA103 itself.

3.5 The evidence relied upon by the trial court to convict the applicant was as follows:

- Anthony Gauci's evidence that the purchaser of the items resembled the applicant "a lot".
- Evidence from various sources that Mr Gauci sold the items on 7 December 1988, a date on which the applicant was proved to be in Malta staying in a hotel close to Mary's House.
- Evidence that on 20-21 December 1988 the applicant was in

Malta travelling on a "coded" passport (i.e. a passport in a false name issued by the Libyan passport authority); and that on 21 December 1988 he was at Luqa airport at a time when baggage for flight KM180 was being checked in.

- Evidence that in 1985 the applicant was a member of the Libyan intelligence service ("JSO", later named "ESO") and until January 1987 was head of the airline security section of that organisation.

- Evidence of the applicant's association with Mr Bollier and with various members of the JSO and Libyan military who purchased MST-13 timers from him.

4.0 Main grounds that were rejected by the Commission

4.1 The following is a summary of some of the Commission's main findings on the grounds of review which were not accepted by the Commission, and accordingly do not form part of the grounds of referral.

- In the initial application to the Commission, reference was made to a former police officer who, it was alleged, worked at a senior level in the police investigation and could provide "sensitive" information about the case. A number of the allegations made on behalf of the applicant were based on information apparently provided by this witness. The true identity of the witness was not disclosed in the application; instead, a pseudonym, "the Golfer", was used. The Commission's enquiry team interviewed the Golfer, a former detective sergeant, on three separate occasions during which he made a number of allegations concerning the conduct of the police investigation. As a result of its enquiries the Commission is satisfied that the Golfer was involved in the police investigation into the bombing of PA103. However, there was a vast array of inconsistencies and contradictions between, and sometimes within, his statements to the Commission. There were also inconsistencies between what he told the Commission and what the submissions alleged he had told the applicant's former legal representatives. In addition the Commission considered some of his allegations to be implausible when considered alongside other evidence in the case, and unsupported or refuted when viewed in the context of the Commission's other findings (see below). In light of this the Commission has serious misgivings as to the credibility and reliability of this witness and was not prepared to accept his allegations.

- Many of the initial and additional submissions received on behalf of the applicant sought to challenge the origin of various items which the trial court accepted were within the primary suitcase. The items in question consisted of a Slalom-make shirt, a pair of Yorkie-make trousers, a babygro and the instruction manual relating to the Toshiba radio cassette player used to conceal the explosive device. To some extent the submissions were based upon allegations said to have been made by the Golfer. Underlying each of them was a suspicion about the conduct of the investigating authorities who, it was alleged, had manipulated, altered or fabricated statements, productions and other records in order to make out a case against the applicant. The Commission conducted extensive investigations into each of the allegations and is satisfied there is no proper basis for any of them. The allegations were further undermined by records recovered by the Commission from the Forensic Explosives Laboratory.

- The additional submissions also sought to cast doubt on the origin of a fragment of circuit board recovered by forensic scientists which the trial court accepted had been part of the MST-13 timer that triggered the bomb. Underlying those submissions was the allegation that evidence of the timer fragment had been fabricated in order to implicate Libya in the bombing. The Commission undertook extensive enquiries in this area but found nothing to support that allegation or to undermine the trial court's conclusions in respect of the fragment.

- Various materials were submitted to the Commission in connection with the evidence given at trial by Mr Allen Feraday, one of the forensic scientists involved in the case. It was pointed out that the Court of Appeal in England had overturned a number of convictions which had been based, at least in part, on Mr Feraday's evidence. The Commission examined papers relating to each of the cases and is satisfied that the evidence given by Mr Feraday on those occasions was different in nature from that which he gave at the applicant's trial. Furthermore, Mr Feraday's evidence concerning the origins of the timer fragment was largely supported by experts instructed by the defence prior to the trial.

- A substantial number of allegations were made to the

- Commission regarding the manner in which the applicant was represented by the legal advisers who acted for him at his trial and his appeal against conviction. The allegations were wide-ranging and covered failures to prepare and present the applicant's defence and to advance legal argument on his behalf. As part of its investigations regarding these claims the Commission conducted lengthy interviews with several members of the applicant's former defence team. However, applying the tests which have been set down by the High Court in previous cases dealing with such matters, the Commission did not consider the allegations to be well-founded.

- The Commission also investigated claims that a former police officer who was involved in searches of the area around Lockerbie after the crash had found a "CIA badge" but had been told by colleagues that such items were not to be recorded as evidence. As part of its enquiries into this allegation the Commission interviewed the officer concerned. It also took statements from another officer who it was alleged had been present when the badge was found, and from the senior investigating officer at the time. Both of these witnesses disputed the officer's claims and the Commission's other enquiries established nothing that might support the claims. Accordingly the Commission was not prepared to accept the officer's allegations.

- It was also alleged in the submissions that items found at the scene of the crash had been "spirited away" and that there had been "unofficial CIA involvement" in the recovery and examination of these. One such item was a suitcase belonging to one of the passengers on PA103, Major Charles McKee. Despite extensive enquiries the Commission found no evidence to suggest that anyone other than Scottish police officers came into contact with Major McKee's suitcase at the scene of the crash. The Commission also found no evidence to support the allegation that a hole had been cut in Major McKee's suitcase in order to gain access to its contents.

- Since the time of the bombing numerous allegations have circulated concerning the possible involvement of Khaled Jaafar, a passenger on PA103 who boarded PA103A at Frankfurt. A number of those allegations were repeated in submissions made to the Commission. The results of the Commission's enquiries in this connection provide no support for the claim that Mr Jaafar was involved, wittingly or unwittingly, in the bombing.

5.0 Grounds of referral

5.1 The following is a brief summary of some of the Commission's main findings on the grounds of review which formed the basis of the grounds of referral:

- A number of the submissions made on behalf of the applicant challenged the reasonableness of the trial court's verdict, based on the legal test contained in section 106(3)(b) of the Criminal Procedure (Scotland) Act 1995. The Commission rejected the vast majority of those submissions. However, in examining one of the grounds, the Commission formed the view that there is no reasonable basis in the trial court's judgment for its conclusion that the purchase of the items from Mary's House, took place on 7 December 1988. Although it was proved that the applicant was in Malta on several occasions in December 1988, in terms of the evidence 7 December was the only date on which he would have had the opportunity to purchase the items. The finding as to the date of purchase was therefore important to the trial court's conclusion that the applicant was the purchaser. Likewise, the trial court's conclusion that the applicant was the purchaser was important to the verdict against him. Because of these factors the Commission has reached the view that the requirements of the legal test may be satisfied in the applicant's case.

- New evidence not heard at the trial concerned the date on which the Christmas lights were illuminated in the area of Sliema in which Mary's House is situated. In the Commission's view, taken together with Mr Gauci's evidence at trial and the contents of his police statements, this additional evidence indicates that the purchase of the items took place prior to 6 December 1988. In other words, it indicates that the purchase took place at a time when there was no evidence at trial that the applicant was in Malta.

- Additional evidence, not made available to the defence, which indicates that four days prior to the identification parade at which Mr Gauci picked out the applicant, he saw a photograph of the applicant in a magazine article linking him to the bombing. In the Commission's view evidence of Mr Gauci's exposure to this photograph in such close proximity to the parade undermines the reliability of his identification of the applicant at that time and at the trial itself.

- Other evidence, not made available to the defence, which the Commission believes may further undermine Mr Gauci's identification of the applicant as the purchaser and the trial court's finding as to the date of purchase.

6.0 Interests of justice test

6.1 Before referring a case to the High Court the Commission must be satisfied not only that a miscarriage of justice may have occurred but also that it is in the interests of justice that a reference be made.

6.2 In determining whether it was in the interests of justice to refer the case the Commission considered a range of matters. These included the various statements which the applicant gave to his legal representatives before the trial in which he set out his position in respect of the allegations against him. It also included the statements which the applicant gave to the Commission. Although there were a number of inconsistencies and contradictions in these accounts, the Commission did not consider the contents of these statements justified the refusal of the case in the interests of justice.

6.3 The Commission also took into account a letter submitted by Libya to the United Nations Security Council in 2003 in which it accepted "responsibility for the actions of its officials" in the "Lockerbie incident". However, as the Commission did not view the letter as amounting to confirmation by Libya of the applicant's guilt, it did not believe that its terms justified refusing his case in the interests of justice.

6.4 Accordingly, the Commission has now referred the case of the applicant to the High Court of Justiciary.

7.0 Media Speculation over the last 3 years

7.1 The Commission has refrained from commenting publicly upon the many articles and stories which have appeared in the press and media during the time of its review of this case. It is fair to say however that much of the information that has been written about the Commission's investigations has been either inaccurate or incorrect. This can only have been upsetting to many of the parties involved in this matter, including the applicant, witnesses at the trial and the families of the victims.

7.2 As recently as within the last week there has been a great deal of media speculation about what is contained within the Commission's statement of reasons, and the reasons for a referral. The Commission is satisfied that the confidentiality of both its enquiries, and the content of its statement of reasons have remained entirely secure during the whole of the review period, and that there has been no leakage of information from within the organisation. Many of the press reports published during the review have simply involved a repetition of certain of the original defence submissions received by the Commission at the beginning of its review, and which have formed the basis of a large part of the Commission's investigation. As indicated in this release, the Commission has concluded after full and proper investigation that these submissions are unsubstantiated and without merit. In particular the Commission has found no basis for concluding that evidence in the case was fabricated by the police, the Crown, forensic scientists or any other representatives of official bodies or government agencies.

7.3 The Commission hopes that, by providing additional information in its short summary of some of the grounds of review and of the conclusions reached, this will end some of these inaccurate reports. The statement of reasons obviously deals with all of these matters in substantially greater detail.

Other information

8.0 The total cost of reviewing the case to date has been £1,108,536. The majority of costs have been in relation to office accommodation, investigation costs including travel, staff salaries and fees of Board members. The breakdown of cost on an annual basis is as follows:

Year Cost
2003-04 £41,000
2004-05 £274,892
2005-06 £361,562
2006-07 £369,785
2007-08 (Anticipated) £61,297
Total £1,108,536

Please note: no further comment will be made by the Commission on the case.

Second appeal (2007 - 2009)

The second appeal was to have been heard by five Scottish judges in 2009 at the Court of Criminal Appeal. A procedural hearing at the Appeal Court in Edinburgh took place on 11 October 2007 when prosecution lawyers and Megrahi's defence Counsel, Maggie Scott QC, discussed legal issues with a panel of three judges. One of the issues concerns a number of CIA documents that were shown to the prosecution but were not disclosed to the defence. The documents are understood to relate to the Mebo MST-13 timer that allegedly detonated the PA103 bomb. Further procedural hearings were scheduled to take place between December 2007 and June 2008.

In September 2008, following an application made at a closed hearing of the Appeal Court in Edinburgh, it was reported that a security-vetted Defence Counsel is to be appointed to examine the disputed document. The court's decision on the application has not been published but in a letter seen by BBC Scotland, FCO minister Kim Howells says it has decided to appoint a special defender.

On 15 October 2008, five Scottish judges decided unanimously to reject a submission by the Crown Office that the scope of Megrahi's second appeal should be limited to the specific grounds of appeal that were identified by the SCCRC in June 2007. On 21 October 2008 Megrahi's lawyer, revealed that his client had been diagnosed with "advanced stage" prostate cancer. Despite the appeals , that keeping Megrahi behind bars while he battled the disease "would amount to exquisite torture", the High Court ruled on 14 November 2008 that Megrahi should remain in jail while his appeal continued.

In January 2009, it was reported that, although Megrahi's second appeal against conviction was scheduled to begin on 27 April 2009, the hearing could last as long as 12 months because of the complexity of the case and volume of material to be examined. On 18 August 2009, Megrahi dropped his appeal in light of his terminal prostate cancer.

Release (2009)

On 20 August 2009, Scotland's Justice Minister, Kenny MacAskill, announced the release of Megrahi under terms of Scottish laws permitting the early release on compassionate grounds of prisoners with less than three months to live. The Scottish authorities and Megrahi's lawyers cited as grounds Megrahi's terminal prostate cancer. In order to facilitate his release Megrahi abandoned his appeal.

After his release from Greenock Prison in Scotland, Megrahi travelled in a white police van flanked by police cars to Glasgow Airport, where he boarded a special V.I.P.-configured Airbus plane from Libya's *Afriqiyah Airways*. Megrahi flew home to Tripoli, Libya, accompanied by Saif al-Islam Muammar al-Gaddafi, son of the Libyan leader, Muammar al-Gaddafi and to what was to be a hero's welcome.

Statistics

Some general statistics:

- there were 84 court days (between 3 May 2000 and 31 January 2001)
- 230 witnesses gave evidence
- the Crown listed 1160 witnesses and called 227

- the defence listed 121 and called 3
- witnesses came from the UK, USA, Libya, Japan, Germany, Malta, Switzerland, Slovenia, Sweden, the Czech Republic, India, France and Singapore
- languages translated in court were Arabic, French, Czech, Japanese, Swedish, Maltese and German
- there were 1867 documentary reproductions and 621 label productions (or *exhibits* - the largest of which was an aircraft reconstruction)
- the aircraft reconstruction was the only one not conveyed to court (it remained at the Air Accident Investigations Branch premises at Farnborough in England)
- there were 10,232 pages of court transcripts covering more than three million words
- the cost of the trial itself was estimated at £60m
- the running costs of the appeal were put at about £2m per month, which combined to produce a total bill of £75m, as estimated by the Scottish Executive
- 20% of the running costs were met by Scotland's Justice Department
- 80% of the running costs along with capital expenditure were borne by the UK government
- the US government made a substantial contribution towards the extra costs of holding the trial in the Netherlands
- the creation of the special court and prison complex at Camp Zeist cost £12m
- original estimates for the entire proceedings were put at £150m (or double the actual spend)
- compensation of £4.5 million ($8 million) was paid in August 2003 by Libya to each family of the 270 victims: a total of £1.23 billion ($2.16 billion)
- contingency fees of £1.4 million ($2.5 million) were deducted from each family's compensation payment, and were retained by the US law firms involved: a total of £385 million ($675 million) in legal fees

Editor's Note

The fact that Megrahi was granted a second appeal is an indication that possibly mistakes were made. The "weak" points in the case are easy to spot:

1. **The route of the suitcase**

   To check-in a suitcase without a passenger is next to impossible on almost any airport. To check in a suitcase *without* passenger for a flight with two changes of aircraft (in Frankfurt and in London) is absolutely impossible.

   Another point is that a terrorist who wants to blow up an aircraft never would choose such a route. It is too complicated and risky. Possible delays (technical/weather) could make it totally unreliable when the bomb would explode and how could he be sure that the bomb is in the right place and that puts the effect of the bomb in serious doubt. The best point in this case would be London Heathrow, the break-in in the bagage department is a clear indication that there was something going on.

2. **The timer**

   The confession of Ultrich Lumpert, the MEBO employee, that he had lied at the trial about the timer, made an end to all speculations that there was something wrong with the value of the timer-evidence. As evidence the timer is now useless. Hereby the Lybian-connection disappears. The fact that his confession came on 18 July 2007 means that it was **not** taken into account by the evaluation of the SCCRC.
   See also appendix A.

3. **Payments to witnesses**

   A number of witnesses (Tony Gauci, Giaka) were paid or promised to be paid (Edwin Bollier) millions of dollars that would link Libya to the case.

Based on the above a second appeal would almost certainly have led to the acquittal of Megrahi. This would be an immense problem because either a new investigation had to take place or the case would have to be abandoned. Releasing Megrahi on compassionate grounds meant that he had to withdraw his request for a second appeal. In other words Megrahi would for ever remain the bomber.

But weather or not with the release of Megrahi, and the abondonning of his appeal, the Lockerbie case is closed remains an open question. There are a number of people, among others Dr. Jim Swire, whose daughter Flora was killed in the Lockerbie bombing, who wants the truth to prevail.

Colonel Qadaffi and oil

Often it is suggested that the key to all is oil. Libya has one of the largest oil reserves of the world. This oil is located far away from the Middle East, close to Europe and the USA, and of an excellent quality. Large parts of the Libyan territory is still unresearched for oil. In other words not only Europe, but also the USA, had a great interest in developing Libyan oil. However, Libya's oil was badly hurt by the UN and US sanctions. There had to be a way to free Libya's oil. This could only be done by bringing Libya back in the world of civilized states. Libya gave already up its nuclear aspirations, by letting Libya admit its role in Lockerbie the road would be cleared for Libyan oil. In an age of skyrocketing oil prices a deal was easy at hand. Libya paid the Lockerbie victims, but never admitted publicly its role in the bombing. The release of Megrahi was the key to the solution.

Colonel Qadaffi is the worlds longest reigning head of state, he survived many American presidents. There is, however, an unsolved problem. In the American air raid on Libya of 1986 Qadaffi's adopted daughter Hannah was killed. For a bedouin moslim this is an unforgivable issue, sooner or later this will blow up in the face of the Americans.

APPENDIX A

Criminal Complaint regarding the Falsification Evidence In the Lockerbie Case

Legal document from the Swiss Law Firm Neupert + Partners sent to the Procurator Fiscal in Dumfries Published as received July 12, 2000 incl. spelling errors, underlining, italics etc.
Hardcopies available - at receivers expenses !
For details, contact aoude@hotmail.com or neupert@nplaw.ch

NEUPERT & PARTNER Rechtsanwalte
Attorney's at law Avocats

<u>Registered</u>

Office of the Procurator Fiscal
Sheriff Courthouse
Buccleuch-Street Dumfries DC-1 2 AN
Scottland
United Kingdom
Zollikon-Zurich July 11, 2000
SA13294.TXT
Criminal Complaint regarding the Falsification Evidence In the Lockerbie Case

Dear Mr Procurator

Acting on behalf of
Mr Edwin Bollier
Badenerstrasse 414, CH-8004 Zurich/Switzerland

a key witness in the case against

Abdelbaset Ali Mohmed Al Megrahi and Al Amin Khalifa Fhimah

we herewith respectfully submit the present request to open

CRIMINAL PROCEEDINGS

with regard to the following punishable offences:

A. Use of a forged (never functioning) fragment of an alleged MST-13 timer, allegedly manufactured by Mebo Ltd.. the company of Mr Edwin Bollier as key evidence for the Crown.

B. . Manipulation with and disfigurement of the alleged MST-13 timer fragment up to September 13, 1999.

C. Total disfigurement of said fragment from September 13, 1999 until June 2000, in order to obliterate shape and colour of said fragment.

REASONING

1. MEBO AG fabricated 3 pieces of brown MST-13 timer motherboards in the middle of 1985. Of these handmade motherboards 2 pieces were subjected to electronic counterparts, thus creating 2 functioning MST-13 timer prototypes. Those were handed over to the Institute for Technical Research (IYTU - STASI/NVA) in Bernau (ex.DDR) in the middle of 1985. The third brown motherboard has allegedly been broken in the hands of the employee Engineer U. Lumpert and disposed of ? (Police protocol testimony, U. Lumpert November 1990, Legal Aid, USA, Scotland).

Also the blueprint for construction of such MST?13 timer prototypes did presumably disappear in the spring of 1990 from MEBO AG.

2. Additionally, 20 pieces of MST-13 timer were fabricated 1985-1986 and delivered to the Libyan military-security in Tripoli Libya. Those MST-13 timers were fitted with

machine-created motherboards, colour: green (Thuring motherboards).

3. It showed that the colour of the alleged Lockerbie-found "Corpus Delicti" would have been of utmost importance for the Scottish Police, in order to identify the origin of the fragments:, one brown fragment. Pol, No. PT/35(b), from a MST13 timer.

4. Why ? The trace tracked back from the Scottish Police to the USA, to the FBI-forensic expert Mr Thomas Thurman. A Scottish forensic expert, Mr. Feraday, did bring the future alleged Lockerbie-found MST-13 timer fragment to the USA, to Thomas Thurman, FBI forensic expert. He then found that the fragment came from a MST- 13 timer, that looks like MST-13 timers, seized from a Libyan courier in Togo and Senegal.

Thomas Thurman then on June 15, 1990 did decide and found that the alleged Lockerbie-found fragment come from a MST- 13 timer, that activated that "Radio-Recorder-Bomb. IED" in the plane of PanAm 103! Thus the link between Lockerbie and Libya was established and on November 14, 1991 the responsibility of the PanAm 103 attack could be transferred to Libya.

The first forensic pictures and films that came from the FBI-laboratory of forensic expert Thomas Thurman clearly contain that the allegedly Lockerbie found fragment came from a brown MST-13 prototype-timer. (Thus the central piece of evidence that the prosecution is relying upon, was in the beginning a brown fragment, from a non-functioning prototype MST-13 timer that was later switched with a green copied fragment-copy!)

5. The then employed MEBO-employee, Engineer U. Lumpert, testified according to the Swiss Legal Aid in the

protocol of November 1990 that he knew that the two MST-13 prototype timers were delivered to the DDR (read testimony from BBC).

Today the investigational administratives claim the police protocol does not contain any such testimony from Lumpert?

Perhaps FBI-forensic expert Thomas Thurman realized - after re-checking with Mr Lumpert - that it was not possible to connect the brown MST-13 prototypetimer with Libya as no brown MST-13 timers were delivered to Libya! - A green MST- 13 timer fragment was to be fetched! It is evident for the two witnesses Mr Meister and Mr Bollier (MEBO) that the present shown forensic evidence pictures of Thurmans as shown in Court in Camp Zeist assumingly belong to computer-photo-edited-pictures that are supposed to point towards green fragments!

6. What are the main points of differences between the BROWN and the GREEN MST? 13 timer fragments ?

   a. The brown motherboard-fragment is 0,4 mm shorter than the green motherboard.

   b. The rounded cut (wedge) on the motherboard has been sawed out by hand on the brown prototype-fragment (saw-structure).

   c. On the green fragment the rounded cut has been milled perfectly (smooth milled structure).

   d. The rounded wedges on the brown and green MST-13 timers are unable to cover each other synchronically (the radius of the wedges are different).

e. The soldering lines on the green motherboard (Thuring board) are perfectly and precisely drawn, yet on the hand-made brown motherboard they are un-precisely and badly soldered-, the copper-lines partially did not accept the tin solder etc.

f. The brown motherboard was cut in two pieces, allegedly for reasons of forensic investigation, The larger part has been labelled evidence No. PT/31 (a), the smaller port No. PT/35(b), Why is the second part not labelled the following No. PT/32(b)? Is it possible to deduce there might exist further (b)-fragments ?

7. When police photographs were added to the Swiss Police protocols as evidence In 1990 at the first inquiry (Legal Aid USA/UK), the pictures showed among other an alleged Lockerbie-found MST-13 fragment that come from a brown MST-13 prototype! During the witness examination In Camp Zeist June 16, 2000, E. Bollier was allegedly shown original protocols from the Swiss Police. Now on envelope was added to the protocols, containing about 5 pictures from FBI-forensic expert Thomas Thurman, E, Bollier had not seen those photographs before even though an appendix with the signature of E, Bollier was added to the envelope. E. Bollier had signed such appendixes for several evidential items. Fact is, there existed no pictures of the brown MST-13 timer fragments added to the allegedly original Swiss protocols in November 1990 signed by Bollier; the pictures must have been switched with similar ones for unknown reasons!

8. From September 15, 1999, after 8 years, finally the gentlemen Meister, Bollier as well as Lumpert from MEBO, could view and inspect the allegedly Lockerbie-found original MST-13 timer fragment during a questioning session in Dumfries Scotland with Principal Procurator Fiscal/Depute Procurator Fiscal Ms Miriam Watson/Mr Harvie.

It was kept on a protocol record from the Police in Dumfries that E. Bollier viewed and inspected a green MST-13 fragment with evidence number PT/31 (a). This fragment was enamelled with green colour, shining and the right part inclusive the rounded cut looked as if treated and cut by loser. At the distinguished soldering-point - the part where a small relais would have been soldered if this would have been a functioning timer - it showed clearly that there never had been soldered any relais. No structural changes were visible at the soldering point! Also, the fragment was 0,4 mm shorter, i.e. it showed the same size as the brown prototyp-fragment that FBI-forensic expert Thomas Thurman on June 15, 1990 presented as the "Lockerbie-fragment" ! The second part of the fragment - labelled Evidence No. PT/35(b) - was brown, just as a prototype MST-13 timer board! Mr Bollier insisted that a police witness confirmed the two motherboards No. PT/31(a)9 and No. PT/35(b) - the socalled "Lockerbie fragments" - had two different colours, (green and brown) !

PROOF:

Statement of Witness by E. Bollier dated 16.09.1999 (enclosure 1)

Statement of Witness by E. Bollier dated 17.09.1999 (enclosure 2)

Statement of Witness by Ms Mirian Watson, Principal Procurator

Fiscal Depute Statement of Witness by Ms Kathrin Thomsen. Det. Insp. Dumfries

Thus something is unambiguously wrong! The witness, Ms Kathrin Thomsen, Det. Insp. Dumfries was called about; she should be able to confirm the two different colours. On

Mr Bolliers's question whether someone from the forensic team had cut a side strip of the fragment PT/31 (a), Principal Procurator Ms Watson answered: in that case the sawed piece should be present too. Consequently there existed at the time no sawed piece, neither was it known that the forensic team hod lost something!

9. When E. Bollier/MEBO on June 14, 2000 in Camp Zeist testified and was examined in Court, he demanded to view the two alleged MST-13 timer fragments once more in their original shapes in order to compare them with the evidential photographs.

10.

After some protests/resistance from the side of the prosecution, the alleged MST-13 fragments PT31 (a) and PT/(b) were put on a table for Mr Bolliers's inspection, What Mr Bollier then sow was criminal: the green fragment No, PT/31 (a) had been altered/manipulated since his lost inspection on September 14, 1999 at the Procurator Ms Watson in Dumfries The evidence was treated with fire. The green lacquer on the motherboard was now lustreless, so was the shining cut, Also the soldering point looked like a "cold" soldering point: now it 'is probably impossible to find out whether any relais was soldered to it. The second piece of fragment No. PT/35(b) that was still a small block on September 14, 1999, still showed some brown colour and was scolded a little by fire on the lower part of its side. hod been altered/manipulated even more. That piece of evidence was totally burnt, it did not show any block shape anymore, it is a thin, curved block piece of "charcoal" that does not show any traces of brown colour. Also, during the evident manipulation, one did not count in the thought that the fragment consisted of one piece, How could the piece PT/35(b) have been burnt completely, while the PT/31 (a) did not show any burning on the sawed ends?

The piece PT/35(b) does not fit anymore to the

ends/cuttings of the PT/31 (b). On that issue, Mr Bollier was lectured by the prosecution that the missing cut port (of the PT/31 (a) was cut off by the police and was lost, This cannot be accounted to forensic testing since it makes no difference whether one end was 0.4 mm shorter, it is still the some end part, The question remains open: should the totally manipulated/changed alleged "Lockerbie-fragment" of a MST-13 still be allowed to act as evidence-MEBO AG . through its lawyers has to file a criminal complaint at the Principal Procurator Fiscal in Dumfries against unknown persons in he forensic-squad of the Scottish Police on reasons of counterfeiting of an important piece of evidence in the biggest criminal case in the world.

10. MEBO has noted that the investigation authorities do not follow the US-evident trail of evidence track leading to the FBI-forensic expert Thomas Thurman with much persistence, Also. Thomas Thurman declared in a television-interview on Channel 4 on November 1998 that he had only viewed the fragment on a photographic image from the Scottish Police; - yet we have learnt from the witness Mr Feraday on June 8, 2000, in Camp Zeist that Feraday had brought the "Lockerbie-fragment" to the FBI in the USA and not a photographic image, Here Thomas Thurman is seemingly lying. During an intern investigation of the FBI it was established that Thomas Thurman had forged evidence in other criminal cases, he was eventually dismissed on the spot by the FBI.

11. Another question Still stands. Why is the Crown in Camp Zeist reluctant to investigate the important evidence whether the explosion occurred outside container AVE 4041 PA ?" is she (the Crown) afraid of the outcome It is a fact that one of the best known explosion-experts, Professor Dr, W, Schubert from the Fraunhofer Institute in Germany, has declared that the investigational authorities are acting on the false premises, that the explosion did not occur inside

the container. Also MEBO and their specialists stand by that fact: - that explosion did not occur inside container AVE 4041 PA. With a relative small financial share the Fraunhofer Institute under the leadership of Prof, Dr. Schuberg and with the aide of other international explosive-experts could prove., no explosion inside Container AVE 4041 PA !

12. Summary: MEBO thinks that the Lockerbie-disaster has been abused to conspire against Libya and has used the firm MEBO as its link. In order to stray further away from the truth, the future "march-heading" is load towards the Middle East (over the PFLG-GC towards Syria and Iran). As the former German Democratic Republic (DDR) and its past State Security Service (STASI) don´t exist anymore, it is a convenient situation for those in charge of the "strategy of politics" to make the DDR-connections responsible for internation terrorism. The defence team (Duff) has shown at the beginning of the proceedings at Camp Zeist whom the hot "Lockerbie-potato" is intended for. MEBO thinks, supported by his (i,e, MEBO's) far-reaching investigation that the PanAm 103-attack was intended for Major Charles McKee and his intelligence-people (US-National Security). Additionally the PanAm 103 disaster can be viewed for different purposes. An alleged Toshiba-Radio bomb inside a Samsonite suitcase was neither loaded in Malta nor in Frankfurt and then transferred to PanAm 103. The explosive detonate was presumably placed directly in Heathrow between container AVE 40AI PA and the fuselage wall of the aircraft on position 700. The plan almost ended perfectly would all the "domino-bricks" have fallen on to each other. Unexpected changes during the countdown of the PanAm-crime leads to the conclusion that one cannot blame Libya to be responsible for the greatest crime in th world.

Would you be so kind as to let me know if you need a formal power of attorney signed by Mr Bollier.

Looking forward to hearing from you, I remain,

Yours sincerely (signed)

Dr. Dieter W. Neupert
(signed In his absence by Andreas Hauri, Attorney at Law)

Other Air Crash Investigations:

On 31 May 2009, flight AF447, an Airbus A330-200, took off from Rio de Janeiro bound for Paris. At 2 h 10, a position message and some maintenance messages were transmitted by the ACARS automatic system. After this nothing was heard of from the aircraft. Six days later bodies and airplane parts were found by the French and Brazilian navies. All 228 passengers and crew members on board are presumed to have perished in the accident. A massive search by air and sea craft for the plane's black boxes failed so far.

On Sunday, March 27, 1977 KLM Flight 4805 and PANAM Flight 1736 both approached Las Palmas Airport in the Canary Islands, when a terrorist's bomb exploded on the airport. Both flights were diverted to the neighboring island of Tenerife. After Las Palmas Airport reopened first KLM Flight 4805 was cleared for takeoff, a few minutes later PANAM 1736 was cleared. Due to a number of misunderstandings both aircraft collided on the runway of Tenerife Airport during takeoff, killing 583 people.

On 1 January 2007, a Boeing 737-4Q8, operated by Adam Air as flight DHI 574, was on a flight from Surabaya, East Java to Manado, Sulawesi, at FL 350 (35,000 feet) when it suddenly disappeared from radar. There were 102 people on board.. Nine days later wreckage was found floating in the sea near the island of Sulawesi. The black boxes revealed that the pilots were so engrossed in trouble shooting the IRS that they forgot to fly the plane, resulting in the crash that cost the lives of all aboard.

278

On February 12, 2009, about 2217 eastern standard time, Colgan Air, Flight 3407, a Bombardier DHC-8-400, on approach to Buffalo-Niagara International Airport, crashed into a residence in Clarence Center, New York, 5 nautical miles northeast of the airport. The 2 pilots, 2 flight attendants, and 45 passengers aboard the airplane were killed, one person on the ground was killed, and the airplane was destroyed. The National Transportation Safety Board determined that the probable cause of this accident was a pilot's error.

On 25 February 2009 a Boeing 737-800, flight TK1951, operated by Turkish Airlines was flying from Istanbul in Turkey to Amsterdam Schiphol Airport. There were 135 people on board. During the approach to the runway at Schiphol airport, the aircraft crashed about 1.5 kilometres from the threshold of the runway. This accident cost the lives of four crew members, and five passengers, 120 people sustained injuries. The crash was caused by a malfunctioning radio altimeter and a failure to implement the stall recovery procedure correctly.

On November 12, 2001, American Airlines flight 587, an Airbus A300-605R, took off from John F. Kennedy International Airport, New York. Flight 587 was a scheduled passenger flight to Santo Domingo, Dominican Republic, with a crew of 9 and 251 passengers aboard the airplane. Shortly after take-off the airplane lost its tail, the engines subsequently separated in flight and the airplane crashed into a residential area of Belle Harbor, New York. All 260 people aboard the airplane and 5 people on the ground were killed, and the airplane was destroyed by impact forces and a post crash fire.

AIR CRASH INVESTIGATIONS

THE CRASH OF AIR FRANCE FLIGHT 358

How an Airbus 340 overrun the runway of Toronto Airport, stopped in a ravine and caught fire, while all passengers and crew members miraculously evacuated the aircraft on time

Hans Griffioen, editor

On August 2, 2005 Air France Flight 358, an Airbus A340, departed Paris, on a flight to Toronto, Canada, with 297 passengers and 12 crew members on board. On final approach, the aircraft's weather radar was displaying heavy precipitation. The aircraft touched down 3800 feet down the runway, and was not able to stop before the end of it. The aircraft stopped in a ravine and caught fire. All passengers and crew members were able to evacuate the aircraft on time. Only 2 crew members and 10 passengers were seriously injured during the crash and the evacuation.

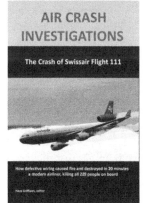

AIR CRASH INVESTIGATIONS

The Crash of Swissair Flight 111

How defective wiring caused fire and destroyed in 20 minutes a modern airliner, killing all 229 people on board

Hans Griffioen, editor

On 2 September 1998, Swissair Flight SR 111 departed New York, flight to Geneva, Switzerland, with 215 passengers and 14 crew members on board. About 53 minutes after departure, the flight crew smelled an abnormal odour in the cockpit. They decided to divert to the Halifax International Airport. They were unaware that a fire was spreading above the ceiling in the front area of the aircraft. They did not make it to Halifax, 20 minutes later the aircraft crashed in the North Atlantic near Peggy's Cove, Nova Scotia, Canada. There were no survivors, 229 people died in the incident.

AIR CRASH INVESTIGATIONS

The Crash of Comair Flight 5191

How Comair Flight 5191, a Bombardier CL-600-2B19, took off from the wrong runway of Blue Grass Airport, Lexington, Kentucky, and crashed, killing 49 passengers and crewmembers

On August 27, 2006, Comair Flight 5191, a Bombardier CL-600-2B19, crashed during takeoff from the wrong runway of Blue Grass Airport, Lexington, Kentucky, killing 49 of the 50 people aboard. From the beginning everything went wrong. First the captain and first officer boarded the wrong airplane, only after starting the auxiliary power unit they found out they were in the wrong aircraft. Taxiing to the takeoff position the captain and first officer were so engaged in a private conversation that they did not realize they took the wrong runway. The air traffic controller did not notice anything.

On 14 August 2005, a Boeing 737-300 aircraft departed from Larnaca, Cyprus, for Prague. As the aircraft climbed through 16.000 ft, the Captain contacted the company Operations Centre and reported a problem. Thereafter, there was no response to radio calls to the aircraft. At 07:21 h, the aircraft was intercepted by two F-16 aircraft of the Hellenic Air Force. They observed the aircraft and reported no external damage. The aircraft crashed approximately 33 km northwest of the Athens International Airport. All 121 people on board were killed.

On 14 September 2008 Aeroflot Flight 821, a Boeing 737-505, operated by Aeroflot-Nord, a subsidiary of the Russian airline Aeroflot, crashed on approach to Bolshoye Savino Airport, Perm, Russia. All 82 passengers and 6 crew members were killed. The aircraft was completely destroyed. According to the final investigation report, the main reason of the crash was pilot error. Both pilots had lost spatial orientation, lack of proper training, insufficient knowledge of English and fatigue from lack of adequate rest. Alcohol in the Captain's blood may also have contributed to the accident.

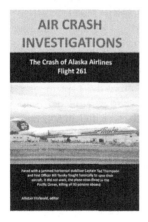

On January 31, 2000, Alaska Airlines, Flight 261, a McDonnell Douglas MD-83, was on its way from Puerto Vallarta, Mexico, to Seattle, Washington, when suddenly the horizontal stabilizer of the plane jammed. Captain Thompson and First officer Tansky tried to make an emergency landing in Los Angeles. The plane suddenly crashed into the Pacific Ocean, killing all 93 people aboard. The NTSB concluded that the crash was caused by insufficient maintenance. The crash of Alaska Airlines Flight 261 could have been avoided.

On May 11, 1996, at 1413:42 eastern daylight time, a Douglas DC-9-32 crashed into the Everglades 10 minutes after takeoff from Miami International Airport, Miami, Florida. The airplane was being operated by ValuJet Airlines, Inc., as flight 592 and was on its way to Atlanta, Georgia. Both pilots, the three flight attendants, and all 105 passengers were killed. The NTSB determined that the cause of the accident, was a fire in the airplane's cargo compartment, initiated by the actuation of an oxygen generator being improperly carried as cargo.

On August 24, 2001, Air Transat Flight 236, an Airbus 330, was on its way from Toronto, Canada to Lisbon, Portugal with 306 people on board. Above the Atlantic Ocean, the crew noticed a dangerous fuel imbalance. After flying 100 miles without fuel the crew managed to land the aircraft at the Lajes Airport at 06:45. Only 16 passengers and 2 cabin-crew members received injuries. The investigation uncovered a large crack in the fuel line of the right engine, caused by mistakes during an engine change just before the start of the flight.

On 19 December 1997 SilkAir Flight 185, a Boeing 737-300, operated by SilkAir, Singapore, on its way from Jakarta to Singapore, crashed at about 16:13 local time into the Musi river near Palembang, South Sumatra. All 97 passengers and seven crew members were killed. Prior to the sudden descent from 35,000 feet, the flight data recorders suddenly stopped recording at different times. There were no mayday calls transmitted from the airplane prior or during the rapid descent. The weather at the time of the crash was fine.

AIR CRASH INVESTIGATIONS

HORROR IN GUAM

The Crash of Korean Air Flight 801

Korean Air Flight 801, a Boeing 747, crashed at Nimitz Hill, on the Island of Guam, because of fatigue of the captain and inadequate flight crew training. The crash killed 228 of the 254 people aboard.

Igor Korovin, editor

On August 6, 1997, about 0142:26 Guam local time, Korean Air flight 801, a Boeing 747-300, crashed at Nimitz Hill, Guam. The aircraft was on its way from Seoul, Korea to Guam with 237 passengers and a crew of 17 on board. Of the 254 persons on board, 228 were killed. The airplane was destroyed by impact forces and a post-crash fire. The National Transportation Safety Board determined that the probable cause of the accident was captain's fatigue and Korean Air's inadequate flight crew training.